ISLINGTON LIBRARIES

3 0120 02233197 9

D0243703

Cambridge First Certificate in English 1

WITH ANSWERS

Official examination papers from University of Cambridge ESOL Examinations

CAMBRIDGE
UNIVERSITY PRESS

CAMBRIDGE UNIVERSITY PRESS
Cambridge, New York, Melbourne, Madrid, Cape Town, Singapore, São Paulo, Delhi

Cambridge University Press
The Edinburgh Building, Cambridge CB2 8RU, UK

www.cambridge.org
Information on this title: www.cambridge.org/9780521714501

© Cambridge University Press 2008

It is normally necessary for written permission for copying to be obtained *in advance* from a publisher. The candidate answer sheets at the back of this book are designed to be copied and distributed in class. The normal requirements are waived here and it is not necessary to write to Cambridge University Press for permission for an individual teacher to make copies for use within his or her own classroom. Only those pages which carry the wording '© UCLES 2008 Photocopiable ' may be copied.

First published 2008
Reprinted 2008

Printed in the United Kingdom at the University Press, Cambridge

A catalogue record for this publication is available from the British Library

ISBN 978-0-521-714501 Student's Book with answers
ISBN 978-0-521-714440 Student's Book without answers
ISBN 978-0-521-714525 Set of 2 Audio CDs
ISBN 978-0-521-714518 Self-study Pack

ISLINGTON LIBRARIES	
Askews	13-Feb-2009
	£32.15
428.24	

Contents

Thanks and acknowledgements   *4*

Introduction   *5*

Test 1	Paper 1	Reading	*8*
	Paper 2	Writing	*14*
	Paper 3	Use of English	*16*
	Paper 4	Listening	*22*
	Paper 5	Speaking	*28*

Test 2	Paper 1	Reading	*30*
	Paper 2	Writing	*36*
	Paper 3	Use of English	*38*
	Paper 4	Listening	*44*
	Paper 5	Speaking	*50*

Test 3	Paper 1	Reading	*52*
	Paper 2	Writing	*58*
	Paper 3	Use of English	*60*
	Paper 4	Listening	*66*
	Paper 5	Speaking	*72*

Test 4	Paper 1	Reading	*74*
	Paper 2	Writing	*80*
	Paper 3	Use of English	*82*
	Paper 4	Listening	*88*
	Paper 5	Speaking	*94*

Test 1	Paper 5 frames	*95*
Test 2	Paper 5 frames	*98*
Test 3	Paper 5 frames	*101*
Test 4	Paper 5 frames	*104*

Marks and results   *107*

Test 1	Key and transcript	*116*
Test 2	Key and transcript	*130*
Test 3	Key and transcript	*144*
Test 4	Key and transcript	*157*

Visual materials for Paper 5   *colour section*

Sample answer sheets   *171*

Thanks and acknowledgements

The authors and publishers acknowledge the following sources of copyright material and are grateful for the permissions granted. While every effort has been made, it has not always been possible to identify the sources of all the material used, or to trace all copyright holders. If any omissions are brought to our notice, we will be happy to include the appropriate acknowledgements on reprinting.

For the article on p. 8, 'Meet the amazing Watkins family' by Matthew Rye, *Daily Telegraph*, 1 July 1999, © Telegraph Group Limited; for the adapted text on p. 10, 'The Kingfisher', *BBC Wildlife Magazine*, April 1998, © Bristol Magazines Ltd; for the extract on p. 13, 'My line of work', *Marie Claire UK*, September 1998, © European Magazines Limited; for the text on p. 30, from *A Patchwork Planet* by Anne Tyler, published by Chatto and Windus. Reprinted by permission of The Random House Group Ltd; for the text on p. 35, adapted from 'Boys of Summer' by Marie-Claire Dorking, *Company Magazine*, August 2001, © The National Magazine Company; for the text on p. 52, from 'Flat in Ringsend' from *Dublin 4* by Maeve Binchy, published by Century. Reprinted by permission of The Random House Group Ltd; for the text on p. 54, 'Ready Steady-Wait by Mary Brown, *Writing Magazine*, June–July 2000. By permission of the author; for the adapted text on p. 57, 'A place to call home' by Nicole Swengley, *The Times*, 8 May 1999, and for the text on p. 19, adapted from 'Play the Game' by Keith Wheatley, *The Times*, 18 May 1997, © N I Syndication; for the text on p. 74, from 'Beyond the Pale' by William Trevor, *Ireland: Selected Stories*, Penguin Books. 1972. Reprinted by permission of PFD on behalf of William Trevor; for the extract on p. 76, adapted from 'In Their Natural Habitat', *Radio Times*, 21–27 March 1998, © BBC Magazines Ltd; for the text on p. 78, adapted from 'Unusual Jobs', *Geographical Magazine*, June 1997, October 1996, December 1995, © Circle Publishing; for the adapted extract on p. 63, from William F Hornby, Melvyn Jones, *An Introduction to Population Geography*, 1993. By permission of Cambridge University Press; for the adapted text on p. 82, 'The World's Shops' by Brian J Knapp from *The World's Changing Energy Supplies (World Geography Series)*, 1994. By permission of Atlantic Europe Publishing Company Ltd.

Colour section
Alamy/Bubbles Photo Library p. C3 (tr); Alamy/David R Frazier Photolibrary Inc p. C7 (br); Alamy/Don Tonge p. C3 (c); Alamy/Eric James p. C13 (t); Alamy/Images of Birmingham p. C7 (t); Alamy/Imagestate p.C5 (t); Alamy/Kevin Foy p. C8 (b); Alamy/Sally & Richard Greenhill p. C2 (t); Alamy/Suzanne Long p. C7 (bl); Arctic Photo/Bryan Alexander p. C3 (b); Corbis/Adam Woolfitt p. C13 (b); Corbis/Eric Gaillard/Reuters p. C16 (t); Corbis/Mango Productions p. C2 (c); Corbis/Steven Vidler/Eurasia Press p. C6 (br); Corbis/Tibor Bognar p. C6 (t); Getty Images/Alfrendo p. C16 (b); Getty Images/Iconica p. C4 (t); Getty Images/Photonica p. C2 (bl); Getty Images/Riser p. C12 (t); Getty Images/Samba Photo p. C7 (c); Getty Images/Stone p. C4 (b); Getty Images/Stone p. C5 (b); Getty Images/Stone p. C12 (b); Getty Images/UpperCut p. C2 (9r); Imagestage/Rob Gage p. C3 (tl); Mark Goebel/Painet/Photographers Direct p. C9 (b); Punchstock p. C1 (b); Punchstock/Digital Vision p. C6 (bl); Punchstock/Photodisc p. C8 (t); Punchstock/Stockbyte p. C1 (t); Robert Harding Picture Library/Roy Rainford p. C9 (t);

Black and white section
Punchstock/Pixtal p. 10; Yves Tzaud/Photographers Direct p. 32

Picture research by Alison Prior

Design concept by Peter Ducker

Cover design by Dunne & Scully

The recordings which accompany this book were made at Studio AVP, London.

Introduction

This collection of four complete practice tests comprises papers from the University of Cambridge ESOL Examinations First Certificate in English (FCE) examination; students can practise these tests on their own or with the help of a teacher.

The FCE examination is part of a suite of general English examinations produced by Cambridge ESOL. This suite consists of five examinations that have similar characteristics but are designed for different levels of English language ability. Within the five levels, FCE is at Level B2 in the Council of Europe's *Common European Framework of Reference for Languages: Learning, teaching, assessment*. It has also been accredited by the Qualifications and Curriculum Authority in the UK as a Level 1 ESOL certificate in the National Qualifications Framework. The FCE examination is widely recognised in commerce and industry and in individual university faculties and other educational institutions.

Examination	Council of Europe Framework Level	UK National Qualifications Framework Level
CPE Certificate of Proficiency in English	C2	**3**
CAE Certificate in Advanced English	C1	2
FCE First Certificate in English	B2	1
PET Preliminary English Test	B1	Entry 3
KET Key English Test	A2	Entry 2

Further information

The information contained in this practice book is designed to be an overview of the exam. For a full description of all of the above exams including information about task types, testing focus and preparation, please see the relevant handbooks which can be obtained from Cambridge ESOL at the address below or from the website at: www.CambridgeESOL.org

University of Cambridge ESOL Examinations
1 Hills Road
Cambridge CB1 2EU
United Kingdom

Telephone: +44 1223 553997
Fax: +44 1223 553621
e-mail: ESOLHelpdesk@ucles.org.uk

The structure of FCE: an overview

The FCE examination consists of five papers.

Paper 1   Reading   1 hour
This paper consists of **three parts,** each containing a text and some questions. Part 3 may contain two or more shorter related texts. There are **30 questions** in total, including multiple-choice, gapped text and multiple-matching questions.

Paper 2   Writing   1 hour 20 minutes
This paper consists of **two parts** which carry equal marks. In Part 1, which is **compulsory,** candidates have to write either a letter or an email of between 120 and 150 words. In Part 2, there are four tasks from which candidates **choose one** to write about. The range of tasks from which questions may be drawn includes an article, an essay, a letter, a report, a review and a short story. The last question is based on the set books. These books remain on the list for two years. Look on the website, or contact the Cambridge ESOL Local Secretary in your area for the up-to-date list of set books. The question on the set books has two options from which candidates **choose one** to write about. In this part, candidates have to write between 120 and 180 words.

Paper 3   Use of English   45 minutes
This paper consists of **four parts** and tests control of English grammar and vocabulary. There are **42 questions** in total. The tasks include gap-filling exercises, word formation and sentence transformation.

Paper 4   Listening   40 minutes (approximately)
This paper consists of **four parts**. Each part contains a recorded text or texts and some questions, including multiple-choice, sentence completion, and multiple-matching. Each text is heard twice. There is a total of **30 questions**.

Paper 5   Speaking   14 minutes
This paper consists of **four parts**. The standard test format is two candidates and two examiners. One examiner takes part in the conversation while the other examiner listens. Both examiners give marks. Candidates will be given photographs and other visual and written material to look at and talk about. Sometimes candidates will talk with the other candidates, sometimes with the examiner and sometimes with both.

Grading

The overall FCE grade is based on the total score gained in all five papers. Each paper is weighted to 40 marks. Therefore, the five FCE papers total 200 marks, after weighting. It is not necessary to achieve a satisfactory level in all five papers in order to pass the examination. Certificates are given to candidates who pass the examination with grade A, B or C. A is the highest. D and E are failing grades. All candidates are sent a Statement of Results which includes a graphical profile of their performance in each paper and shows their relative performance in each one.

For further information on grading and results, go to the website (see page 5).

Test 1

PAPER 1   READING (1 hour)

Part 1

You are going to read a newspaper article about a musical family. For questions **1–8**, choose the answer (**A**, **B**, **C** or **D**) which you think fits best according to the text.

Mark your answers **on the separate answer sheet**.

Meet the Amazing Watkins Family

The sons are composers and prize-winning musicians, while Dad makes the instruments.
Matthew Rye *reports.*

Whole families of musicians are not exactly rare. However, it is unusual to come across one that includes not only writers and performers of music, but also an instrument maker.

When South Wales schoolteachers John and Hetty Watkins needed to get their ten-year-old son, Paul, a cello to suit his blossoming talents, they baulked at the costs involved. 'We had a look at various dealers and it was obvious it was going to be very expensive,' John says. 'So I wondered if I could actually make one. I discovered that the Welsh School of Instrument Making was not far from where I lived, and I went along for evening classes once a week for about three years.'

line 17 'After probably three or four goes with violins and violas, he had a crack at his first cello,' Paul, now 28, adds. 'It turned out really well. He made me another one a bit later, when he'd got the hang of it. And that's the one I used right up until a few months ago.' John has since retired as a teacher to work as a full-time craftsman, and makes up to a dozen violins a year – selling one to the esteemed American player Jaime Laredo was 'the icing on the cake'.

Both Paul and his younger brother, Huw, were encouraged to play music from an early age. The piano came first: 'As soon as I was big enough to climb up and bang the keys, that's what I did,' Paul remembers. But it wasn't long before the cello beckoned. 'My folks were really quite keen for me to take up the violin, because Dad, who played the viola, used to play chamber music with his mates and they needed another violin to make up a string trio. I learned it for about six weeks but didn't take to it. But I really took to the character who played the cello in Dad's group. I thought he was a very cool guy when I was six or seven. So he said he'd give me some lessons, and that really started it all off. Later, they suggested that my brother play the violin too, but he would have none of it.'

'My parents were both supportive and relaxed,' Huw says. 'I don't think I would have responded very well to being pushed. And, rather than feeling threatened by Paul's success, I found that I had something to aspire to.' Now 22, he is beginning to make his own mark as a pianist and composer.

Meanwhile, John Watkins' cello has done his elder son proud. With it, Paul won the string final of the *BBC Young Musician of the Year* competition. Then, at the remarkably youthful age of 20, he was appointed principal cellist of the BBC Symphony Orchestra, a position he held, still playing his father's instrument, until last year. Now, however, he has acquired a Francesco Rugeri cello, on loan from the Royal Academy of Music. 'Dad's not said anything about me moving on, though recently he had the chance to run a bow across the strings of each in turn and had to admit that my new one is quite nice! I think the only thing Dad's doesn't have – and may acquire after about 50–100 years – is the power to project right to the back of large concert halls. It will get richer with age, like my Rugeri, which is already 304 years old.'

Soon he will be seen on television playing the Rugeri as the soloist in Elgar's Cello Concerto, which forms the heart of the second programme in the new series, *Masterworks*. 'The well-known performance history doesn't affect the way I play the work,' he says. 'I'm always going to do it my way.' But Paul won't be able to watch himself on television – the same night he is playing at the Cheltenham Festival. Nor will Huw, whose String Quartet is receiving its London premiere at the Wigmore Hall the same evening. John and Hetty will have to be diplomatic – and energetic – if they are to keep track of all their sons' musical activities over the coming weeks.

1   Why did John Watkins decide to make a cello?

    A   He wanted to encourage his son Paul to take up the instrument.
    B   He was keen to do a course at the nearby school.
    C   He felt that dealers were giving him false information.
    D   He wanted to avoid having to pay for one.

2   What is meant by 'crack' in line 17?

    A   attempt
    B   plan
    C   shock
    D   period

3   What do we learn in the third paragraph about the instruments John has made?

    A   He considers the one used by Jaime Laredo to be the best.
    B   He is particularly pleased about what happened to one of them.
    C   His violins have turned out to be better than his cellos.
    D   It took him longer to learn how to make cellos than violins.

4   Paul first became interested in playing the cello because

    A   he admired someone his father played music with.
    B   he wanted to play in his father's group.
    C   he was not very good at playing the piano.
    D   he did not want to do what his parents wanted.

5   What do we learn about Huw's musical development?

    A   His parents' attitude has played little part in it.
    B   It was slow because he lacked determination.
    C   His brother's achievements gave him an aim.
    D   He wanted it to be different from his brother's.

6   What does Paul say about the Rugeri cello?

    A   His father's reaction to it worried him.
    B   The cello his father made may become as good as it.
    C   It has qualities that he had not expected.
    D   He was not keen to tell his father that he was using it.

7   What does Paul say about his performance of Elgar's Cello Concerto?

    A   It is less traditional than other performances he has given.
    B   Some viewers are likely to have a low opinion of it.
    C   He considers it to be one of his best performances.
    D   It is typical of his approach to everything he plays.

8   What will require some effort from John and Hetty Watkins?

    A   preventing their sons from taking on too much work
    B   being aware of everything their sons are involved in
    C   reminding their sons what they have arranged to do
    D   advising their sons on what they should do next

Part 2

You are going to read an article about a bird called the kingfisher. Seven sentences have been removed from the article. Choose from the sentences **A–H** the one which fits each gap (**9–15**). There is one extra sentence which you do not need to use.

Mark your answers **on the separate answer sheet**.

The kingfisher

Wildlife photographer Charlie James is an expert on the kingfisher: a beautiful blue-green bird that lives near streams and rivers, feeding on fish.

Old trees overhang the stream, half shading shallow water. Soft greens, mud browns and the many different yellows of sunlight are the main colours, as soft as the sounds of water in the breeze. The bird cuts like a laser through the scene, straight and fast, a slice of light and motion so striking you almost feel it. It has gone in a split second, but a trace of the image lingers, its power out of proportion to its size.

Charlie James fell in love with kingfishers at an early age. **9** After all, it is the stuff of legend. Greek myth makes the kingfisher a moon goddess who turned into a bird. Another tale tells how the kingfisher flew so high that its upper body took on the blue of the sky, while its underparts were scorched by the sun.

10 For despite the many different blues that appear in their coats, kingfishers have no blue pigment at all in their feathers. Rather, the structure of their upper feathers scatters light and strongly reflects blue.

11 It's small wonder that some wildlife photographers get so enthusiastic about them. Couple the colours with the fact that kingfishers, though shy of direct human approach, can be easy to watch from a hideout, and you have a recipe for a lifelong passion.

Charlie James's first hideout was an old blanket which he put over his head while he waited near a kingfisher's favourite spot. **12** But it took another four years, he reckons, before he got his first decent picture. In the meantime, the European kingfisher had begun to dominate his life. He spent all the time he could by a kingfisher-rich woodland stream.

The trouble was, school cut the time available to be with the birds. So he missed lessons, becoming what he describes as an 'academic failure'. **13**

At 16, he was hired as an advisor for a nature magazine. Work as an assistant to the editor followed, then a gradual move to life as a freelance wildlife film cameraman. What he'd really like to do now is make the ultimate kingfisher film. **14** 'I'm attracted to the simple approach. I like to photograph parts of kingfisher wings ...'

The sentence trails off to nothing. He's thinking of those colours of the bird he's spent more than half his life getting close to, yet which still excites interest. **15** But, as Charlie knows, there's so much more to his relationship with the kingfisher than his work can ever show.

A This is why a kingfisher may appear to change from bright blue to rich emerald green with only a slight change in the angle at which light falls on it.

B But his interest in this, the world's most widespread kingfisher and the only member of its cosmopolitan family to breed in Europe, was getting noticed.

C A sure sign of his depth of feeling for this little bird is his inability to identify just what it is that draws him to it.

D The movement sends a highly visible signal to rivals, both males and females, as it defends its stretch of water against neighbours.

E The bird came back within minutes and sat only a metre away.

F The photographs succeed in communicating something of his feelings.

G 'No speech, just beautiful images which say it all,' he says.

H There is some scientific truth in that story.

Part 3

You are going to read a magazine article in which various people talk about their jobs. For questions **16–30**, choose from the people (**A–D**). The people may be chosen more than once.

Mark your answers **on the separate answer sheet**.

Which person says their job involves

large amounts of paperwork?	**16**
training high-level staff in their area of work?	**17**
taking measures to protect public safety?	**18**
accepting certain financial limitations?	**19**
encouraging visitor participation?	**20**
listening to disagreements?	**21**
doing considerable background research?	**22**
introducing problems that require solutions?	**23**
balancing supply and demand?	**24**
producing advertising literature?	**25**
organising trips designed to increase people's awareness?	**26**
constant updating of their own materials?	**27**
corresponding with the public?	**28**
working in an area that has personal meaning for them?	**29**
working with a team of colleagues?	**30**

My line of work

Four people talk about their jobs.

A Lisa – Exhibition Programmes Organiser, Science Museum

I'm responsible for putting temporary exhibitions together. This includes planning and designing the exhibition and promoting it. I have to read up about the subject of the exhibition beforehand and then talk to important people in the area so that I can establish the main themes and aims of the exhibition, and plan what objects and pictures should be displayed. I have to make sure the public can understand the thinking behind the exhibition, which means planning interactive displays, workshops and theatre. I also have to bring in engineers and electricians to make sure the final display is not dangerous to visitors. Before the exhibition opens, I help design and write the brochures and leaflets that we'll use to tell people about it.

B Janet – Teacher of London Taxi Drivers

The first thing I do when I get here at 7.30 a.m. is check the accounts. Then I see what new maps and documents need to be produced in order to learn the 'runs' or routes necessary to pass the London taxi-driver test. By midday, about 50 students are in school, working out how to make the journeys. They work out the most direct route, using the correct one-way streets, and right- and left-hand turns. I get involved when there's a difference of opinion – like whether you can do a right turn at a particular junction. When they're close to the test, I'll give them a simple route and no matter what way they say they'll go, I'll tell them they have to use another route because the road is closed. The next student will have to find a third route and again I'll come up with a reason why they can't go that way. It's just to make them think.

C Sarah – Marine Conservationist

I live by the coast and work from home. This involves responding to telephone enquiries, producing educational resources and setting up training courses. Occasionally, I go into our main office but generally I am on the coast. I also work with schools and study centres and run courses for coastal managers and those involved in making decisions about the fate of the seas. I do things like take them out to sea in a boat in an attempt to make them think more about the life underneath them. This often changes their views as it's very different from making decisions using a computer screen. I am extremely lucky because conservation is my hobby, so the job has many highs for me. The downside of the job is that I work for a charity, so there is a constant need for more money. This means I'm always looking for more resources and I'm not able to achieve everything I want.

D Chris – Map and Atlas Publisher

My work is pretty varied. I have to make sure that the publishing programme matches market requirements, and ensure that we keep stocks of 300 or so of the books that we publish. We have very high standards of information and content. We receive many letters from readers on issues such as the representation of international boundaries and these in particular require a careful response. I discuss future projects and current sales with co-publishers. I work as part of an enthusiastic group which makes the job that much more enjoyable. The negative side, as with many jobs, is that there is far too much administration to deal with, which leaves less time to work on the more interesting tasks such as product development and design.

13

PAPER 2   WRITING (1 hour 20 minutes)

Part 1

You **must** answer this question. Write your answer in **120–150** words in an appropriate style.

---

1   You are planning to visit your friend Robin in Canada. Robin has written to you. Read Robin's letter and the notes you have made. Then write a letter to Robin, using **all** your notes.

My friends and I are going to a sports camp in the mountains in July. We'd love you to join us there. We can play tennis, hockey, football, basketball and other sports. We can stay in rooms or sleep in tents. Which would you prefer? We'll cook together in the evenings. Is there something special from your county that you could cook?

You could fly over to Canada a few days before the sports camp and stay with me here in the city. What would you like to do before we go to the camp?

Write soon.

Robin

Great because...

Say which and why

Yes! Explain...

Tell Robin

Write your **letter**. You must use grammatically correct sentences with accurate spelling and punctuation in a style appropriate for the situation.

Do not write any postal addresses.

Part 2

Write an answer to **one** of the questions 2–5 in this part. Write your answer in **120–180** words in an appropriate style.

2   You see this advertisement in an English language newspaper.

INTERNATIONAL BOOKSHOP REQUIRES SUMMER STAFF

- Do you like books and reading?
- Do you speak English?
- Do you have any useful experience?

Apply to the manager, Mrs Benson, saying why you think you are suitable for a job in our international bookshop.

Write your **letter of application**. Do not write any postal addresses.

3   You recently saw this notice in an international entertainment magazine.

Reviews needed!

We are starting a new section in the magazine called 'Great TV Programmes around the World'. Could you write a **review** of your favourite TV programme for this section? In your review, say what kind of programme it is, what happens in the programme and why you like it so much.

The best reviews will be published in the magazine.

Write your **review**.

4   You have decided to enter a short story competition in an international magazine. The story must **begin** with the following words:

Alison read the note, smiled, and immediately put on her coat.

Write your **story**.

5   Answer **one** of the following two questions based on **one** of the titles below.

(a) *The Citadel* by A. J. Cronin
On several occasions in *The Citadel* Andrew Manson meets a person who deliberately makes life difficult for him. Write an **essay** describing one of these situations and saying how Andrew deals with it.

Write your **essay**.

(b) *Around the World in 80 Days* by Jules Verne
This is part of a letter from your English-speaking penfriend.

Having read 'Around the World in 80 Days', it's easy to see that travelling was more enjoyable in the days before the invention of the aeroplane – don't you agree?

Write a **letter** to your penfriend giving your opinion. Do not write any postal addresses.

Write your **letter**.

PAPER 3 USE OF ENGLISH (45 minutes)

Part 1

For questions **1–12**, read the text below and decide which answer (**A**, **B**, **C** or **D**) best fits each gap. There is an example at the beginning (**0**).

Mark your answers **on the separate answer sheet**.

Example:

0   **A** believe   **B** imagine   **C** realise   **D** suppose

0	A	B	C	D
	—	▬	—	—

PAPER

'Just **(0)** ..... a day without paper,' reads one advertisement for a Finnish paper company. It adds, 'You almost **(1)** ..... see our products every day.' And they're right. But in most industrial countries, people are so **(2)** ..... to paper – whether it's for holding their groceries, for drying their hands or for **(3)** ..... them with the daily news – that its **(4)** ..... in their daily lives passes largely unnoticed.

At one **(5)** ..... paper was in short supply and was used mainly for important documents, but more recently, growing economies and new technologies have **(6)** ..... a dramatic increase in the **(7)** ..... of paper used. Today, there are more than 450 different grades of paper, all designed for a different **(8)** ..... .

Decades ago, some people predicted a 'paperless office'. **(9)** ....., the widespread use of new technologies has gone hand-in-hand with an increased use of paper. Research into the relationship between paper use and the use of computers has shown that the general **(10)** ..... is likely to be one of growth and interdependence.

However, the costs **(11)** ..... in paper production, in terms of the world's land, water and air resources, are high. This **(12)** ..... some important questions. How much paper do we really need and how much is wasted?

1	**A**	positively	**B**	obviously	**C**	certainly	**D**	absolutely
2	**A**	conscious	**B**	acquainted	**C**	familiar	**D**	accustomed
3	**A**	providing	**B**	delivering	**C**	contributing	**D**	giving
4	**A**	task	**B**	operation	**C**	service	**D**	role
5	**A**	time	**B**	instance	**C**	date	**D**	occasion
6	**A**	called on	**B**	come around	**C**	brought about	**D**	drawn up
7	**A**	total	**B**	portion	**C**	number	**D**	amount
8	**A**	point	**B**	goal	**C**	purpose	**D**	result
9	**A**	Instead	**B**	Besides	**C**	Otherwise	**D**	Alternatively
10	**A**	method	**B**	order	**C**	trend	**D**	system
11	**A**	involved	**B**	contained	**C**	held	**D**	connected
12	**A**	puts	**B**	raises	**C**	gets	**D**	places

Part 2

For questions **13–24**, read the text below and think of the word which best fits each gap. Use only **one** word in each gap. There is an example at the beginning (**0**).

Write your answers **IN CAPITAL LETTERS on the separate answer sheet**.

Example: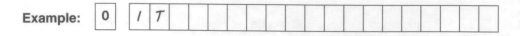

COMPETITION: YOUR IDEAL SCHOOL

Is your school just as you want (**0**) .....it..... to be? Or are there things you and your classmates (**13**) .... change, given the opportunity? This is your chance to express your ideas about (**14**) .... the ideal school is like. Our competition is open to (**15**) .... student between the ages of twelve and eighteen. You can enter (**16**) .... an individual or your whole class can work together on a team entry. Your entry can take any form – a piece of writing, a picture, or even architectural plans. It is completely (**17**) .... to you. What we are looking for is evidence (**18**) .... originality, imagination and, above (**19**) ...., the genuine views of young people.

By (**20**) .... part in this, you will help in a study being carried out at a leading university. All work entered (**21**) .... the competition will be kept at the university and used in research. Entries cannot be returned (**22**) .... of this. But it also means that, even (**23**) .... you do not win, your views will still be heard and will remain for future educationalists to study.

Entries must reach us no later (**24**) .... Friday 30 April. Winners will receive valuable prizes of computer equipment and software for their schools.

Part 3

For questions **25–34**, read the text below. Use the word given in capitals at the end of some of the lines to form a word that fits in the gap **in the same line**. There is an example at the beginning (**0**).

Write your answers **IN CAPITAL LETTERS on the separate answer sheet**.

Example:

0	B	I	T	T	E	R	L	Y									

NEW WATERPROOF CLOTHING

There are few experiences as unpleasant as being (**0**) ....*bitterly*.... cold and   **BITTER**

dripping wet on board a boat. The (**25**) .... that you may be several   **KNOW**

hours away from warm, dry clothing is enough to slow down even the

(**26**) .... sailor.   **TOUGH**

However, recent (**27**) .... developments in the types of material used   **SCIENCE**

to make waterproof clothes have, hopefully, put an end to the (**28**) ....   **SUFFER**

of the sailor. New suits, trousers and jackets have been designed which

allow people to stay warm and dry at sea and can be worn (**29**) ....   **COMFORT**

for days on end.

The new clothing is by no means cheap, but that will not stop it

from selling well, and not just in the sailing market. (**30**) ....   **LIKE**

previous types of waterproof clothing, which tended to leave the

wearer hot, sweaty and sticky even after a (**31**) .... short burst of   **RELATIVE**

(**32**) .... activity, these new clothes are manufactured with an   **ENERGY**

(**33**) .... inner layer. This is made of a special material which allows   **ADDITION**

the clothes to 'breathe' – in other words, body heat can escape so that

the body stays dry, but still maintains its (**34**) .... in all weathers.   **WARM**

Part 4

For questions **35–42**, complete the second sentence so that it has a similar meaning to the first sentence, using the word given. **Do not change the word given**. You must use between **two** and **five** words, including the word given. Here is an example (**0**).

Example:

0   You must do exactly what the manager tells you.

CARRY

You must .... instructions exactly.

The gap can be filled by the words 'carry out the manager's', so you write:

Example: | 0 | *CARRY OUT THE MANAGER'S*

Write **only** the missing words **IN CAPITAL LETTERS on the separate answer sheet**.

---

35   Marcella left home very early because she wanted to be sure of catching the train.

ORDER

Marcella left home very early .... miss the train.

36   You must show your student card as you enter the library.

REQUIRED

You .... student card as you enter the library.

37   On arriving at an airport, I usually go straight to the check-in desk.

SOON

I usually go straight to the check-in desk as .... to an airport.

38   Patrick hadn't heard from his uncle in Australia for over five years.

MORE

It was .... Patrick had heard from his uncle in Australia.

39 On business trips, I prefer driving home to staying in a hotel overnight.

RATHER

On business trips, I'd .... in a hotel overnight.

40 Jack found it difficult to control his skis on the steep slope.

UNDER

Jack found it difficult to .... on the steep slope.

41 They say the fashion model was discovered by her agent while working at a restaurant.

SAID

The fashion model is .... discovered by her agent while working at a restaurant.

42 Such success has not been achieved by many players in the world of ice hockey.

FEW

Only .... such success in the world of ice hockey.

PAPER 4   LISTENING (approximately 40 minutes)

Part 1

You will hear people talking in eight different situations. For questions **1–8**, choose the best answer (**A**, **B** or **C**).

1   You hear a restaurant manager talking about the cooks who work for him.
    What does he say about them?

   A   They dislike cleaning tasks.

   B   They have a choice of jobs.

   C   They help to decide the menu.

2   You hear a woman talking about a new book.
    What does she particularly like about the book?

   A   It is educational.

   B   It is well organised.

   C   It is enjoyable.

3   You hear the writer of a television soap opera being interviewed about the programme.
    What will happen next in the story?

   A   Someone will make an important decision.

   B   Someone will go away unexpectedly.

   C   Someone will learn the truth at last.

4   You hear part of a radio interview.
    Who is speaking?

   A   a taxi driver

   B   a porter

   C   a tourist guide

5 You hear a woman talking about how she keeps fit.
Why did she decide to take up line dancing?

    A   She thought the pace would suit her.

    B   She had heard about it on television.

    C   She wanted to try exercising to music.

6 You overhear a conversation in a restaurant.
What does the woman think about the food she has just eaten?

    A   It was expensive.

    B   It was delicious.

    C   It looked wonderful.

7 You turn on the radio and hear a man talking.
What is he talking about?

    A   drawing pictures

    B   writing fiction

    C   composing music

8 You overhear a student phoning her parents.
What is her opinion of the place she is living in while at college?

    A   She is not sure she will have enough room to study.

    B   She has difficulty in working because of the noise.

    C   She does not get on well with her room-mates.

Part 2

You will hear an interview with Elizabeth Holmes about her experience working in Africa. For questions **9–18**, complete the sentences.

Volunteering in Africa

Elizabeth worked for a [**9**   ] before she went to Africa.

Elizabeth first found out about working as a volunteer from a

[**10**   ] she saw at the dentist's.

The course in London that Elizabeth attended was called [**11**   ]

Elizabeth's job in Africa was to teach

[**12**   ] how to market their goods.

On arrival in Africa, Elizabeth spent

[**13**   ] doing a training course with other volunteers.

Elizabeth used a [**14**   ] to travel short distances in Africa.

Elizabeth feels that she got on best with

[**15**   ] in the area of Africa where she lived.

Back in England, Elizabeth found that she was disturbed by the

[**16**   ] in the city.

At the moment, Elizabeth buys and sells [**17**   ] from Africa.

Nowadays, Elizabeth spends more time on her favourite pastime, which is

[**18**   ]

Part 3

You will hear five different employees talking about what makes a good boss. For questions **19–23**, choose which of the opinions (**A–F**) each speaker expresses. Use the letters only once. There is one extra letter which you do not need to use.

A good boss should

A   allow staff to take decisions.

Speaker 1		19

B   encourage staff to work in teams.

Speaker 2		20

C   listen to complaints from staff.

Speaker 3		21

D   give information on individual progress.

Speaker 4		22

E   have good qualifications.

Speaker 5		23

F   set an example of hard work.

Part 4

You will hear an interview with Trina Trevose, a pop singer who is only fifteen. For questions **24–30**, choose the best answer (**A**, **B** or **C**).

24 When Trina went to the USA, she

    A   thought the records she made would be unsuccessful.

    B   knew her friends would be jealous of her.

    C   didn't tell many people why she was going.

25 When Trina was in the USA, she wrote songs about

    A   her home.

    B   the weather.

    C   people she met.

26 Where was Trina performing when she was noticed by the record company?

    A   in London

    B   near her home

    C   in the USA

27 Why did Trina sing with David Pearson?

    A   He needed some help.

    B   She wrote a song for him.

    C   The record company asked her to.

28 Trina was asked to return to the USA to

    A   re-do some work.

    B   appear on TV again.

    C   record a new song.

29 Why isn't Trina popular in Britain?

    A   Her kind of music isn't popular in Britain.

    B   The company don't want to sell her records in Britain.

    C   Her records haven't been available in Britain.

30 How does Trina see her future?

    A   She will continue making records in the USA.

    B   She may make singing her career eventually.

    C   She wants to study music at college.

PAPER 5   SPEAKING (14 minutes)

You take the Speaking test with another candidate, referred to here as your partner. There are two examiners. One will speak to you and your partner and the other will be listening. Both examiners will award marks.

Part 1 (3 minutes)

The examiner asks you and your partner questions about yourselves. You may be asked about things like 'your home town', 'your interests', 'your career plans', etc.

Part 2 (a one-minute 'long turn' for each candidate, plus 20-second response from the second candidate)

The examiner gives you two photographs and asks you to talk about them for one minute. The examiner then asks your partner a question about your photographs and your partner responds briefly.

Then the examiner gives your partner two different photographs. Your partner talks about these photographs for one minute. This time the examiner asks you a question about your partner's photographs and you respond briefly.

Part 3 (approximately 3 minutes)

The examiner asks you and your partner to talk together. You may be asked to solve a problem or try to come to a decision about something. For example, you might be asked to decide the best way to use some rooms in a language school. The examiner gives you a picture to help you but does not join in the conversation.

Part 4 (approximately 4 minutes)

The interlocutor asks some further questions, which leads to a more general discussion of what you have talked about in Part 3. You may comment on your partner's answers if you wish.

Test 2

PAPER 1   READING (1 hour)

Part 1

You are going to read an extract from a novel. For questions **1–8**, choose the answer (**A, B, C** or **D**) which you think fits best according to the text.

Mark your answers **on the separate answer sheet**.

On the very last day of a bad year, I was leaning against a pillar in the Baltimore railway station, waiting to catch the 10.10 to Philadelphia. There were a lot more people waiting than I had expected. That airy, light, clean, polished feeling I generally got in the station had been lost. Elderly couples with matching luggage stuffed the benches, and swarms of college kids littered the floor with their bags.

A grey-haired man was walking around speaking to different strangers one by one. Well-off, you could tell: tanned skin, nice sweater, soft, beige car-coat. He went up to a woman sitting alone and asked her a question. Then he came over to a girl standing near me. She had long blond hair, and I had been thinking I wouldn't mind talking to her myself. The man said, 'Would you by any chance be travelling to Philadelphia?'

'Well, northbound, yes,' she said.

'But to Philadelphia?'

'No, New York, but I'll be ...'

'Thanks, anyway,' he said, and he moved toward the next bench.

Now he had my full attention. 'Ma'am,' I heard him ask an old lady, 'are you travelling to Philadelphia?' When the woman told him, 'Wilmington,' he didn't say a thing, just marched on down the row to one of the matched-luggage couples. I straightened up from my pillar and drifted closer, looking toward the platform as if I had my mind on the train.

Well, *I* was going to Philadelphia. He could have asked me. I understood why he didn't, of course. No doubt, I struck him as unreliable. He just glanced quickly at me and then swerved off toward the bench at the other end of the waiting area. By now he was looking seriously stressed. 'Please!' he said to a woman reading a book. 'Tell me you're going to Philadelphia!'

She lowered her book. She was thirtyish, maybe thirty-five – older than I was, anyhow. A school-teacher sort. 'Philadelphia?' she said. 'Why, yes, I am.'

'Then could I ask you a favour?'

I stopped several feet away and frowned down at my left wrist. (Never mind that I don't own a *line 27* watch.) Even without looking, I could sense how she went on guard. The man must have sensed it too, because he said, 'Nothing too difficult, I promise!'

They were announcing my train now. People started moving toward Gate E, the older couples hauling their wheeled bags behind them like big pets on leashes. Next I heard the man talking. 'My daughter's flying out this afternoon for a study year abroad, leaving from Philadelphia. So I put her on a train this morning, stopping for groceries afterward, and came home to find my wife in a state. She hardly said "hello" to me. You see my daughter'd forgotten her passport. She'd telephoned home from the station in Philadelphia; didn't know what to do next.'

The woman clucked sympathetically. I'd have kept quiet myself. Waited to find out where he was *line 36* heading with this.

'So I told her to stay put. Stay right there in the station, I said, and I would get somebody here to carry up her passport.'

A likely story! Why didn't he go himself, if this was such an emergency?

'Why don't you go yourself?' the woman asked him.

'I can't leave my wife alone for that long. She's in a wheelchair.'

This seemed like a pretty poor excuse, if you want my honest opinion. Also, it exceeded the amount of bad luck that one family could expect. I let my eyes wander toward the two of them. The man was holding a packet, not a plain envelope, which would have been the logical choice, but one of those padded envelopes the size of a paperback book. Aha! Padded! So you couldn't feel the contents! And from where I stood, it looked to be stapled shut besides. Watch yourself, lady, I said silently.

1   What was the narrator's impression of the station that morning?

    A   People were making too much noise.
    B   It was unusually busy.
    C   There was a lot of rubbish on the ground.
    D   The seating was inadequate.

2   Why does the narrator show an interest in the grey-haired stranger?

    A   He was fascinated by the stranger's questions.
    B   He was anxious about the stranger's destination.
    C   He was jealous of the stranger's appearance.
    D   He was impressed by the stranger's skill with people.

3   What does the writer mean by 'she went on guard' in line 27?

    A   The woman was employed by the railway company.
    B   The woman was ready to call the police.
    C   The woman was surprised by the man's attitude.
    D   The woman was cautious in her response.

4   According to the stranger, how was his wife feeling when he got home?

    A   relieved to see him
    B   annoyed by their daughter's phone call
    C   upset about their daughter's situation
    D   worried about planning the best course of action

5   What does 'this' refer to in line 36?

    A   the story
    B   the passport
    C   the station
    D   the telephone call

6   When the narrator had heard the stranger's explanation, he felt

    A   sympathetic towards the stranger's daughter.
    B   willing to offer his assistance.
    C   doubtful about the combination of events.
    D   confused by the story the stranger told.

7   When the narrator sees the packet, he thinks that the woman should

    A   remain on the platform.
    B   proceed carefully.
    C   ask to check the contents.
    D   co-operate with the man.

8   What do we learn about the narrator's character from reading this extract?

    A   He enjoys talking to strangers.
    B   He has a strong sense of curiosity.
    C   He has a kind-hearted attitude to people.
    D   He interferes in the affairs of others.

Part 2

You are going to read a newspaper article about a board game called 'pichenotte'. Seven sentences have been removed from the article. Choose from the sentences **A–H** the one which fits each gap (**9–15**). There is one extra sentence which you do not need to use.

Mark your answers **on the separate answer sheet**.

Onto a winner

Two brothers are finding that their childhood game is very good for business.

Dave and Norm Lagasse, two bushy-bearded brothers in their forties, are sitting in their modest home in Santa Fe in New Mexico, USA, and reliving their childhood. In front of them lies a wooden board covered in round plastic pieces. They are playing the ancient game of pichenotte, one which, they insist, is unlike any other.

Their grandfather, Lucien Rajotte, a grocer originally from Quebec, Canada, brought the game into the USA and introduced it to his family. It wasn't long before, on just about every weekend and holiday, the family were playing the game and, as Dave says, 'having the best time ever'. Eventually, the family moved to New Mexico. **9** If visitors dropped by they were often fascinated, for the game was completely unknown in southern USA.

One day, three years ago, Dave set up the ancient pichenotte board and, realising how cracked and battered it had become, decided to make a new one. This turned out to be a beauty. A relative noticed and wanted one. Then a friend wanted another. **10** 'People there started to watch,' says Dave, 'and say, "No way I'm playing that silly game." Then they'd sit down, and pretty soon you couldn't get them up from the table!'

11 The roots, he discovered, were probably in India, where a similar game called 'carroms' exists. That was adapted into a game called 'squails' which was played in pubs in Britain and, a century ago, British people emigrating to Canada brought the game with them. Pichenotte is the name of the French-Canadian version of the game that developed in Quebec.

12 Each competitor gets 12 pieces or 'pucks'. These are 'flicked' across a wheel-like board using the middle or index finger of one hand. Flicking a puck into a small hole is worth 20 points. Three concentric rings around the hole are worth 15, 10 and 5, respectively. Eight tiny posts present obstacles. The game usually lasts just two minutes.

When they saw how popular the game was at the Santa Fe bar, the Lagasses made a couple more boards and took them to markets and craft fairs. Crowds gathered, money changed hands and the game's popularity grew. **13** With word spreading more widely, the boards began to sell as fast as the brothers could make them. Eventually, they decided to go into the pichenotte business full-time.

They set up a workshop in the garage of their house and started turning out boards. More than 450 have been produced to date. **14** As Norm explains, 'They're very durable, as they have to stand up to lots of wear.' They are available, at $595 each, from the brothers' website.

As yet, there are no professional pichenotte players or TV coverage to produce pichenotte celebrities. **15** Until then, they're happy to spend their off-duty hours playing the game they hope will make their fortune.

A This idea always brings a smile to the face of Mrs Lagasse, at 70 still an excellent player herself.

B Made of birchwood and mahogany, each weighs 12kg and is 1cm thick.

C Pichenotte, which can be played by two to four people, is clearly a game of skill.

D But Grandpa's pichenotte board, which he'd made out of old wooden food crates, was not forgotten and they continued to play regularly.

E When people started asking about the origins of the game, Dave decided to do some research.

F So much so that championships began to take place and a trophy called the 'Lord Pichenotte Cup' was created.

G Nonetheless, the day is not far off when the brothers' garage will be home to a luxury Mercedes rather than a saw and piles of wood.

H Curious as to how great the interest might be, one night the brothers took one of Dave's new game boards to a sports bar in Santa Fe.

Part 3

You are going to read an article about four sportsmen. For questions **16–30**, choose from the sportsmen (**A–D**). The sportsmen may be chosen more than once.

Mark your answers **on the separate answer sheet**.

Which sportsman mentions

a time-consuming aspect of being well known in his sport?	16	
a career opportunity resulting from an achievement in sport?	17	
the financial rewards of success in his sport?	18	
a good result that went largely unnoticed?	19	
the importance of having a social life outside sport?	20	
enjoying a change of scene when training?	21	
difficulties in a relationship resulting from his lifestyle?	22	
enjoying being recognised by people in the street?	23	
attracting attention for things not directly connected to the sport?	24	
not finding the idea of fame attractive?	25	
regretting having to turn down invitations?	26	
the advantages and disadvantages of supporters coming to watch the sport?	27	
the time of day he has to go training?	28	
disappointment at not getting help as a result of an achievement?	29	
a feeling that his sporting career will be relatively short?	30	

Dedicated to their sports

Four young sports stars talk about their lives.

A   Darius (runner)

I've always been sporty. I played a bit of everything at one time, but I was best at football and athletics. When I was 14, I had a trial for a professional football club, but eventually I opted to go down the athletics route instead. My biggest moment came when I got to compete for my country in the youth team and got a medal. It didn't result in much media attention, though, which was a shame. I'd been hoping some sponsorship would come out of it, because the training doesn't come cheap. I train at home all winter and then go away for three weeks, usually Florida, before the season starts. It's good fun – there are great athletics facilities there and the nightlife's great too. You've got to be really disciplined, though. If friends ask me to go out the night before training, I have to say no. I wish I didn't, but dedication pays in this sport. The main goal for me is to get to the next Olympics – that would be fantastic.

B   Gabriel (surfer)

The surfing community is small, so you get to meet the same guys wherever you compete. Professional surfers are very serious and often the best waves are at dawn, so if you're really going to get anywhere, you have to cut out late-night parties altogether. I don't mind that so much, but I do love having a lie-in, and I usually have to give that up too. But it's worth it, because without that kind of dedication I might not have won the National Championships last year. I make sure that a big night out follows any win, though, and if there's cash involved in the winnings, I'll go away somewhere really nice. And, of course, the sacrifices are worth it in the long run because winning that championship meant I got picked to present a surfing series on TV. I guess I'm a bit of a celebrity now.

C   Dieter (yacht racer)

With five lads on a boat together, you have a good laugh. We're very traditional and we always celebrate a win in great style. It's been said that we act a bit childishly when we're out, but we don't actively go looking for media coverage. Sometimes the reporters actually seem more concerned about where you go out celebrating and what you get up to there than about where you came in the race. I'm away for eight months of the year, so it's great to get back, go out with my mates from other walks of life and do the things they do. You can't live, eat and breathe the sport all the time – it's not healthy. I'm known within the world of sailing, but fortunately I can count the number of times I've been recognised in the street on the fingers of one hand. I'd hate to become some sort of celebrity. I get a lot of nice letters from people wanting signed pictures, though. It may take ages, but I reply to every one. It would be cheeky to complain, even if it does take a bit of organising.

D   Tomas (tennis player)

It's always a great thing to walk on court and feel that the crowd's behind you. At the last tournament, though, it all got a bit crazy with people crowding around. Despite that, I have to admit that I do still get quite a thrill out of being spotted by fans when I'm out shopping or something. It has its downside though. My last girlfriend didn't like it if I got too much attention from female fans. The thing is, tennis players have to travel quite a lot, and in the end that's why we split up, I guess. That was hard, but you've got to make sacrifices in any sport; you've got to be serious and professional. Actually, it doesn't really bother me too much. I'm content to concentrate on my game now and catch up on the other things in life once I've retired, because, after all, that comes pretty early in this sport.

PAPER 2   WRITING (1 hour 20 minutes)

Part 1

You **must** answer this question. Write your answer in **120–150** words in an appropriate style.

---

1   Your English-speaking friend, Sam, is an art student and has written to you with a request.
    Read Sam's email and the notes you have made. Then write an email to Sam, using **all** your
    notes.

---

email

From: Sam
Sent: 18th June
Subject: Art Course

---

*I've recently started an art course and we're doing a
project at the moment called 'People at Home' and our
teacher has asked us to paint someone in their home or
garden. Would you let me come and paint you?*

Yes!

*If so, where would be a good place? I don't mind if it's
indoors or outdoors but could you describe it for me, as
that would help me with my preparation.*

Describe
somewhere
suitable

*Also, I'd like to include a special object in the picture –
something important to you. It doesn't need to be
beautiful or valuable!*

Say what and
why

*Please write back soon if you'd like to be painted.
If you have any questions, just ask.*

Ask about…

Look forward to hearing from you.

Sam

Write your **email**. You must use grammatically correct sentences with accurate spelling and
punctuation in a style appropriate for the situation.

Part 2

Write an answer to **one** of the questions **2–5** in this part. Write your answer in **120–180** words in an appropriate style.

---

2 A group of British students would like to go camping in your area. The group leader has asked you to write a **report** including the following information:

- the best place to camp in your area, and why
- the best time of year for camping there
- what clothes the group members should bring with them.

Write your **report**.

3 Here is part of a letter you have received from an English-speaking friend.

> I'm doing a project at college about how people use the internet these days. I know you enjoy using the internet more than I do so I hope you can help! What's your favourite website? How has the internet changed the way you do things?
>
> Do write soon.

Write to your friend giving your opinion.

Write your **letter**.

4 An international music magazine that you read is looking for reviews with the following title: *'The last CD I bought'*. You decide to write a **review** for the magazine. Describe the music on the CD and say what you think about it. Would you recommend the CD to other people?

Write your **review**.

5 Answer **one** of the following two questions based on **one** of the titles below.

(a) *The Citadel* by A. J. Cronin
You see the following notice in a magazine.

We are looking for articles about relationships in literature. The best articles will be published in this magazine!

Write an **article** for the magazine about the relationship between Andrew Manson and his wife Christine in *The Citadel*.

Write your **article**.

(b) *Around the World in 80 Days* by Jules Verne
In *Around the World in 80 Days* by Jules Verne, Phileas Fogg and his companions have many exciting adventures on their journey around the world.

Write an **essay** saying which adventure you found most exciting and why.

Write your **essay**.

PAPER 3   USE OF ENGLISH (45 minutes)

Part 1

For questions **1–12**, read the text below and decide which answer (**A, B, C** or **D**) best fits each gap. There is an example at the beginning (**0**).

Mark your answers **on the separate answer sheet**.

Example:

0   **A** known   **B** common   **C** popular   **D** normal

0	A	B	C	D
	—	—	▬	—

THE MUSTARD SHOP

Norwich, a city in the east of England, is a **(0)** ..... shopping centre for thousands of people. In particular, visitors love to **(1)** ..... the small, unusual shops hidden away in Norwich's narrow streets. The Mustard Shop is usually high on everybody's **(2)** ..... of interesting shops to see.

The **(3)** ..... between mustard, a type of sauce, and Norwich **(4)** ..... back to the nineteenth century. Jeremiah Colman began to make mustard in 1814 in a nearby village. The yellow fields, full of mustard flowers whose seeds were required for Colman's factory, soon changed the appearance of the local **(5)** ..... . The company **(6)** ..... rapidly and in 1854 it moved to a suburb on the **(7)** ..... of Norwich. By this time, Colman's mustard was famous in many countries. The company is still in **(8)** ..... and many people continue to enjoy eating mustard with meat, cheese and other food.

In 1973, the company opened The Mustard Shop. It is a careful reproduction of a typical mustard shop of a hundred years ago and sells a wide **(9)** ..... of mustards. Upstairs there is a small museum where visitors can **(10)** ..... a collection of old Colman's posters and an exhibition **(11)** ..... the history of mustard. It is a shop not to be **(12)** ..... when visiting Norwich.

1   **A**   explore   **B**   enquire   **C**   research   **D**   analyse

2   **A**   account   **B**   brochure   **C**   list   **D**   guide

3   **A**   join   **B**   tie   **C**   union   **D**   link

4   **A**   comes   **B**   goes   **C**   belongs   **D**   leads

5   **A**   view   **B**   scenery   **C**   background   **D**   nature

6   **A**   expanded   **B**   enlarged   **C**   increased   **D**   strengthened

7   **A**   limits   **B**   frontiers   **C**   sides   **D**   outskirts

8   **A**   reality   **B**   fact   **C**   existence   **D**   force

9   **A**   amount   **B**   extent   **C**   range   **D**   set

10 **A**   review   **B**   watch   **C**   examine   **D**   remark

11 **A**   explaining   **B**   announcing   **C**   expressing   **D**   discovering

12 **A**   unnoticed   **B**   missed   **C**   escaped   **D**   left

Part 2

For questions **13–24**, read the text below and think of the word which best fits each gap. Use only **one** word in each gap. There is an example at the beginning (**0**).

Write your answers **IN CAPITAL LETTERS on the separate answer sheet**.

Example: | 0 | A | M | O | N | G | | | | | | | | | | | | | | |

DICTIONARIES

Dictionaries are **(0)** 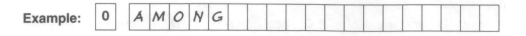 among the most important tools of self-education. **(13)** .... Samuel Johnson wrote his influential English dictionary in the eighteenth century, the work kept him busy for seven years. At the end of that period he **(14)** .... written the meanings of over forty thousand words. Most modern dictionaries require a **(15)** .... deal less time and effort to write because writers often use earlier dictionaries **(16)** .... a source of reference.

Nowadays, most dictionaries are put together by teams of writers, or lexicographers. Sometimes they need to work together in meetings; at other times they work independently of **(17)** .... other, on different parts of the dictionary.

(18) .... one time, the starting point for deciding on which words to include used to be the lexicographer's own knowledge. These days, teams **(19)** .... use of a large collection of examples of **(20)** .... only writing but also everyday speech, which is known as a *corpus*. Teams also refer **(21)** .... books and articles about language as **(22)** .... as asking experts in particular subjects about the more specialised words. Finally, ordinary people are asked to say what they think about the **(23)** .... the words are defined and **(24)** .... they find the examples provided helpful or not.

Part 3

For questions **25–34**, read the text below. Use the word given in capitals at the end of some of the lines to form a word that fits in the gap **in the same line**. There is an example at the beginning (**0**).

Write your answers **IN CAPITAL LETTERS on the separate answer sheet**.

Example:

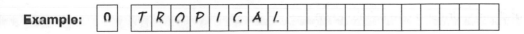

ISLAND IN THE SUN

With its **(0)** ......tropical...... sunshine, clear, blue water and the warm welcome   **TROPIC**
you will receive, this island is hard to beat as a holiday destination.
The island has something for everyone, but the **(25)** .... west coast   **DELIGHT**
is the perfect **(26)** .... for people who love water sports,   **CHOOSE**
such as water-skiing and windsurfing. For those who prefer a more
relaxing holiday, there are beaches of fine, white sand, facing the calm
Caribbean Sea and also an **(27)** .... selection of restaurants,   **IMPRESS**
where the local seafood is **(28)** .... recommended.   **HIGH**

Among the many other **(29)** .... on the island are trips in a submarine –   **ATTRACT**
which allow you to explore the island's fascinating coral reefs – Caribbean
dancing and a jazz festival held **(30)** ...., early in January. It is also worth   **ANNUAL**
travelling along the wild east coast, where, because it faces the Atlantic
Ocean, the weather is often **(31)** .... Sadly, this makes the coast rather   **STORM**
(32) .... for swimming, in contrast to the calmer beaches on the west   **SUITABLE**
coast. Getting round the island is not difficult, as car and bicycle hire is
(33) .... arranged, and there is an excellent road system, with a very   **EASY**
(34) .... bus service.   **RELY**

Part 4

For questions **35–42**, complete the second sentence so that it has a similar meaning to the first sentence, using the word given. **Do not change the word given.** You must use between **two** and **five** words, including the word given. Here is an example (**0**).

Example:

0   A very friendly taxi driver drove us into town.

DRIVEN

We .... a very friendly taxi driver.

The gap can be filled by the words 'were driven into town by', so you write:

Example:	0	*WERE DRIVEN INTO TOWN BY*

Write **only** the missing words **IN CAPITAL LETTERS on the separate answer sheet**.

---

35   My views on this subject are exactly the same as yours.

DIFFERENCE

There .... my views on this subject and yours.

36   Sara knew that her brother had to leave by 5 o'clock.

NECESSARY

Sara knew that .... her brother to leave by 5 o'clock.

37   'What's the height of the mountain?' Lee asked his father.

HIGH

Lee asked his father .... was.

38   The secretary said that they had run out of paper for the photocopier.

LEFT

The secretary said that there wasn't .... for the photocopier.

39 I wished I'd done more to help.

HAVING

I regretted .... more to help.

40 They will be selling tickets for the concert during the lunch hour.

SALE

Tickets for the concert will .... during the lunch hour.

41 We played tennis despite the cold weather.

EVEN

We played tennis .... cold.

42 The manager had the respect of everyone in the office.

UP

Everyone in the office .... the manager.

PAPER 4   LISTENING (approximately 40 minutes)

Part 1

You will hear people talking in eight different situations. For questions **1–8**, choose the best answer (**A**, **B** or **C**).

1   You overhear a woman talking to her husband on a mobile phone.
    What is the background to the conversation?

   A   The family's holiday may have to be cancelled.

   B   The woman wants to buy their son a computer.

   C   Their son has schoolwork to complete before the start of term.

2   You hear a phone-in programme on the radio.
    Why has the man phoned?

   A   to complain about the traffic scheme

   B   to express his support for the traffic scheme

   C   to question the aims of the traffic scheme

3   On the radio, you hear a woman talking about her house.
    What has she recently done?

   A   decided to move to another area

   B   solved a problem that she had

   C   made improvements to her house

4   You overhear two people discussing a friend.
    What language does their friend usually speak at home?

   A   French

   B   English

   C   Italian

5 You hear a man talking about an activity holiday he went on as a child with his family.
How did he feel during the holiday?

A bored by the climbing

B upset with his father

C disappointed with the rowing boat

6 You hear the beginning of a radio programme.
What is the programme going to be about?

A child development

B the environment

C a form of entertainment

7 You hear a man being interviewed about a new project he has set up.
What is the purpose of the project?

A to help people find accommodation in Scotland

B to tell people where to stay in Australia

C to advise people how to set up a flat agency

8 You switch on the radio in the middle of a programme.
What kind of programme is it?

A an arts review

B an interview

C a quiz show

Part 2

You will hear an announcement about an evening's programmes on Radio Pearl. For questions **9–18**, complete the sentences.

7.30 pm 'Art Review': Student Art Exhibition

This evening's programme is taking place at the

| | **9** | in London.
|---|---|

The exhibition is of work by students in the

| | **10** | year of their art course.
|---|---|

At the exhibition, you can see things as different as curtains and

	11

Some of the works of art have been made using

| | **12** | technology.
|---|---|

8.00 pm Play: 'The Vanishing Lady'

In the play, a young couple on a train think they hear the sound of someone using a

	13

A | | **14** | tells the couple about an old lady whom he has seen.

After writing this play, the author, Porten, became a writer for

	15

9.30 pm 'Business Scenes': Interview with Peter Field

Peter used to work for a | | **16** |

Peter says the material he uses for his boats is a particular kind of

	17

Peter collects | | **18** | as a hobby.

Part 3

You will hear five different people talking about the way they study. For questions **19–23**, choose from the list (**A–F**) which of the opinions each speaker expresses. Use the letters only once. There is one extra letter which you do not need to use.

A Music helps me concentrate when I'm studying.

Speaker 1 | **19**

B I study best in the morning when I can think clearly.

Speaker 2 | **20**

C I realise I study better when I'm outside in the open air.

Speaker 3 | **21**

D I find I can concentrate better when I study with a friend.

Speaker 4 | **22**

E It is much easier for me to study late at night.

Speaker 5 | **23**

F I prefer to study when I'm lying down.

Part 4

You will hear a girl called Tricia Simpkins talking at a public meeting about a plan to create a nature reserve in the centre of a large city. For questions **24–30**, choose the best answer (**A, B** or **C**).

---

24 How did Tricia once feel about the countryside?

  A She preferred it to the city.

  B She paid no attention to it.

  C She wanted others to experience it.

25 Why did Tricia take part in a wildlife survey?

  A She was required to do it.

  B She preferred it to being in school.

  C She was asked to do it by her neighbours.

26 What does Tricia say about the results of the survey?

  A They were unsatisfactory.

  B They were confusing.

  C They were unexpected.

27 What does Tricia say about the problems created by trees?

  A People exaggerate them.

  B People ignore them.

  C People accept them.

28 According to Tricia, what is wrong with the trees the council is planting?

  A They are expensive to replace.

  B They fail to attract wildlife.

  C They are too small for the area.

29 What used to happen in the wasteland at the end of Tricia's street?

    A   Dog owners used to go there.

    B   People used to leave rubbish there.

    C   Children used to play there.

30 What is Tricia's suggestion for the new nature reserve?

    A   to allow the planting of trees

    B   to protect it from visitors

    C   to let it go wild

PAPER 5   SPEAKING (14 minutes)

You take the Speaking test with another candidate, referred to here as your partner. There are two examiners. One will speak to you and your partner and the other will be listening. Both examiners will award marks.

Part 1 (3 minutes)

The examiner asks you and your partner questions about yourselves. You may be asked about things like 'your home town', 'your interests', 'your career plans', etc.

Part 2 (a one-minute 'long turn' for each candidate, plus 20-second response from the second candidate)

The examiner gives you two photographs and asks you to talk about them for one minute. The examiner then asks your partner a question about your photographs and your partner responds briefly.

Then the examiner gives your partner two different photographs. Your partner talks about these photographs for one minute. This time the examiner asks you a question about your partner's photographs and you respond briefly.

Part 3 (approximately 3 minutes)

The examiner asks you and your partner to talk together. You may be asked to solve a problem or try to come to a decision about something. For example, you might be asked to decide the best way to use some rooms in a language school. The examiner gives you a picture to help you but does not join in the conversation.

Part 4 (approximately 4 minutes)

The interlocutor asks some further questions, which leads to a more general discussion of what you have talked about in Part 3. You may comment on your partner's answers if you wish.

Test 3

PAPER 1   READING (1 hour)

Part 1

You are going to read an extract from a short story. For questions **1–8**, choose the answer (**A**, **B**, **C** or **D**) which you think fits best according to the text.

Mark your answers **on the separate answer sheet**.

Finding a good flat in Dublin at a price you could afford was like finding gold in the gold rush. The best way was by personal contact: if you knew someone who knew someone who was leaving a place, that often worked. But if, like Jo, you had only just arrived in Dublin, there was no chance of any personal contact, nobody to tell you that *line 5* their bedsit would be vacant at the end of the month. No, it was a matter of staying in a hostel and searching.

For Jo, Dublin was a very big blank spot. She really felt she was stepping into the unknown when she got on the train to go and work there. She didn't ask herself why she was going there in the first place. It had been assumed by everyone she went around with at school that she would go. Who would stay in a one-horse town, the back of beyond, the end of the world, the sticks? That's all she had heard for years. They were all going to get out, escape, see some life, get some living in, have a real kind of existence, and some of the others in her class had gone as far as the towns of Ennis or Limerick, where an elder sister or an aunt would see them settled in. But out of Jo's year, none of them were going to Dublin. She was heading off on her own.

Jo's mother thought it would be great if she stayed permanently in the hostel. It was run by nuns, and she would come to no harm. Her father said that he hoped they kept the place warm; hostels were well known for being freezing. Jo's sisters, who worked in a hotel as waitresses, said she must be off her head to have stayed a whole week in a hostel. But Jo didn't know they were all still thinking about her and discussing her, as she answered the advertisement for a flat in Ringsend. It said, 'Own room, own television, share kitchen, bathroom.' It was very near the post office where she worked and seemed too good to be true. Please, please let it be nice, let them like me, let it not be too dear!

There wasn't a queue for this one because it wasn't so much 'Flat to Let', more 'Third Girl Wanted'. The fact that it said 'own television' made Jo wonder whether it might be too high a class for her, but the house did not look in any way overpowering. An ordinary red-brick terraced house with a basement. But the flat was not in the basement, it was upstairs. And a cheerful-looking girl with a college scarf, obviously a failed applicant, was coming down the stairs. 'Desperate place,' she said to Jo. 'They're both awful. Common as dirt.' 'Oh,' said Jo and went on climbing.

line 31 'Hello,' said the girl with 'Nessa' printed on her T-shirt. 'Did you see that toffee-nosed girl going out? I can't stand that kind, I can't stand them.' 'What did she do?' asked Jo. 'Do? She didn't have to *do* anything. She just poked around and pulled a face and sort of giggled and then said, "Is this all there is to it? Oh dear, oh dear," in a posh accent. We wouldn't have her in here, would we, Pauline?'

Pauline had a psychedelic shirt on, so colourful it almost hurt the eyes, but even so it was only slightly brighter than her hair. Pauline was a punk, Jo noted with amazement. She had seen some of them on O'Connell Street, but hadn't met one close up to talk to. 'I'm Jo, I work in the post office and I rang.' Nessa said they were just about to have a mug of tea. She produced three mugs; one had 'Nessa' and one had 'Pauline' and the other one had 'Other' written on it. 'We'll get your name put on if you come to stay,' she said generously.

1   What does 'it' in line 5 refer to?

   A   the accommodation available
   B   finding accommodation
   C   getting advice on accommodation
   D   the shortage of accommodation

2   What do we learn about Jo's schoolfriends in paragraph 2?

   A   They would have liked to be as independent as Jo was.
   B   They had more self-confidence than Jo had.
   C   They had made Jo feel that she ought to leave her home town.
   D   They were not as happy as Jo was to move to a new town.

3   What impression do we get of Jo's home town?

   A   It was an uninteresting place in the middle of the countryside.
   B   It was a place where peole struggled to earn a living.
   C   It was a place where the population had fallen greatly.
   D   It was an unfriendly place, where young people were treated badly.

4   What did Jo think about the flat in Ringsend before she saw it?

   A   that she was likely to be able to afford it
   B   that the advertisement for it was confusing
   C   that it might not be as suitable for her as it first sounded in the advertisement
   D   that it did not really have all the facilities mentioned in the advertisement

5   What do we learn about the girl who passed Jo on the stairs?

   A   She was upset that she was not going to live in the flat.
   B   She liked neither the flat nor the other girls living there.
   C   She had not been seriously intending to live in the flat before seeing it.
   D   She had not realised that other people were already living in the flat.

6   What is meant by 'toffee-nosed' in line 31?

   A   feeling superior
   B   being curious about others
   C   strange-looking
   D   appearing nervous

7   What did Jo think when she first met Pauline?

   A   She probably wouldn't like Pauline because of her appearance.
   B   Pauline was different from other punks she had met.
   C   Pauline would probably not want to make friends with her.
   D   She knew very little about people who looked like Pauline.

8   By the end of the extract, we learn that

   A   Nessa and Pauline did not really want anyone to share their flat.
   B   other people had moved out of the flat because they had not enjoyed living there.
   C   Nessa felt that Jo would be more suitable than the previous applicant.
   D   Nessa and Pauline were not expecting anyone to want to share their flat.

Part 2

You are going to read a magazine article about how to become a published author. Seven sentences have been removed from the article. Choose from the sentences **A–H** the one which fits each gap (**9–15**). There is one extra sentence which you do not need to use.

Mark your answers **on the separate answer sheet**.

Trying to get published?

If you are wondering where to send your story, our expert Margaret Stubbs is here with the advice you need.

Readers of this magazine often write in saying, 'I have written this story/book. Can you please tell me who to send it to?' One of the first things they need to know is that they should be researching their markets and finding out about publishers as well as practising their writing skills. Turning words into a saleable commodity takes a good deal of knowledge about the 'writing game'.

Whatever kind of writing you do, you need to develop a knowledge of the markets you are aiming at. **9** Use your local library and go round the local bookshops and newsagents. Reading widely will always give you the best guide to what kinds of writing publishers are actually accepting at any given time.

As time goes on, this knowledge must be updated as new publications are constantly appearing – editors change jobs, and magazines change direction. **10** Publishers are always hungry for new blood; as writers we have to make sure we give them what they want.

To begin with you may be looking around, not quite sure what you want to write. Let us say you feel that you might like to write short love stories. The very first thing you must do is find out which magazines use love stories, a rather limited market these days, and get hold of as many recent copies as you can. **11** These readers will expect different things from their magazine, and the editor is only interested in catering to their needs.

Writers often send me their stories saying, 'This has been rejected three times – please tell me if I am wasting my time ... do I stand a chance at all?' **12** But it is unlikely that the work is of publishable standard; so I have to try to give an honest opinion, but always with a positive viewpoint.

The problem is that most new writers are too eager to send their work out, usually long before they are ready to enter the market. If you have only written one story or one article, it is not at all likely to be published. **13** When you read about so-called 'overnight success', you usually find that the person has been in the publishing trade or journalism for some years before their current success.

When you do finally send off some of your work for the first time, immediately get on with more work while you await a reply; write ten more stories, twenty even. Each one will be better than the last, and you will begin to think of yourself as a writer, and both your fluency and your confidence will grow. **14** Also I would advise not showing your work to anyone else, certainly in the early stages.

Don't forget that every successful writer will have had many rejections before succeeding. Do everything you can to advance your career as a writer. See whether there's a creative writing course near you. **15** Think of yourself as a writer and get that writing practice in – every day if possible.

A However, if you fancy yourself as a writer of thrillers then you will need to read books by thriller writers.

B Then familiarise yourself with the kind of stories they are buying, taking special note of who the readers are.

C That almost never happens.

D If not, try joining a local writers' group which will help you to gain ideas and confidence from mixing with other aspiring writers.

E There are several ways of doing this, but the best one is simply by reading everything relevant you can lay your hands on.

F Don't tear any of them up – improve them instead.

G New titles are coming and going all the time.

H As a former teacher, I would never actively discourage anyone.

Part 3

You are going to read a magazine article in which five people talk about their favourite places. For questions **16–30**, choose from the people (**A–E**). The people may be chosen more than once. When more than one answer is required, these may be given in any order.

Mark your answers **on the separate answer sheet**.

Which person or people

appreciates a little luxury?	**16**	
enjoy an area that they appreciated as a child?	**17**	**18**
enjoys watching other people in their everyday lives?	**19**	
appreciates the plantlife in their favourite place?	**20**	
appreciates a lack of noise?	**21**	
like an area which few people visit?	**22**	**23**
revealed talents as a child which were required in their future career?	**24**	
stays in inexpensive accommodation?	**25**	
finds changing circumstances add to their appreciation of the place?	**26**	
admits the landscape is not very special?	**27**	
experienced a variety of landscapes while still a child?	**28**	**29**
has been keen to share their enthusiasm with others?	**30**	

Favourite places

A Bruce

I don't like landscapes which are completely untamed. It's the human element which is important to me. It's the same when I travel abroad. Lovely villages with old temples attract me, not empty deserts. When I was eight, I went away to school in England and on Saturdays I would cycle to the village of Lastingham in its lovely valley. Cycling was a release from school. I loved exploring the bleak hilltops, the sheltered valleys and old villages. Coming from Scotland myself, I found the landscape familiar yet different and I still go back there today. I used to describe my adventures in my private diary. In a way, that was my first attempt at travel writing, at which I subsequently made my name.

B Sophia

There is a miniature railway that goes from Hythe to Dungeness, run by amateurs. I always travel first class as it doesn't cost much more than the regular fare. The scenery is not spectacular. The train moves across Romney Marsh with its sheep, and alongside a canal. But there is one point on the journey that I always look forward to – when our miniature world takes a detour through back gardens. For a few moments, we passengers spy on people at random points in their day, making a cup of tea, doing the washing up, unfolding a deckchair. I see myself in their eyes, a woman in a tiny train carriage, looking into other people's homes. It's the ordinariness of the landscape that attracts me. Just fields and sheep and a distant grey sea. That makes me look more closely, to search for something that opens my eyes.

C Matthew

The Hartland Peninsula is a remote and lovely coast. The beaches are hard to reach and scattered with rocks, so crowds are largely non-existent here. They attract a few brave surfers but most visitors prefer instead to reflect on the majesty of the sea. The coast, which faces the Atlantic, is notorious for shipwrecks. There are coast walks which you can combine with trips inland up beautiful damp valleys, full of oak trees, ferns and wild flowers. We stay in modest self-catering accommodation with a family who have some property in the village of Southole.

D Annette

My favourite place in England is the Trough of Bowland, a landscape of wide-open moorland which is perfect for hiking. There are not many residents and not many visitors either. It's an unknown corner, empty and remote, and I like the feeling of space. I discovered the area by chance when I was a student, and since then I've made an annual visit, either alone, or with my boyfriend, and now with my son. It has changed little since my first visit. Having a child makes these visits more special. It makes me sad that he's growing up in an urban environment.

E James

I purchased Glenthorne, my favourite house in Britain. It was a question of obtaining pure peace and reconnecting with my English roots and coming home. I grew up in what is now known as Sri Lanka, but at the age of twelve went to school in Devon, in the west of England. I used to cycle around the moors and village backstreets. We had a story about a place we would never cycle past: if you went down the driveway you'd never return. That place was Glenthorne. It's the place of my dreams. It's a magic, secluded, romantic house. You can't hear anything except sea, wind and birds.

PAPER 2   WRITING (1 hour 20 minutes)

Part 1

You **must** answer this question. Write your answer in **120–150** words in an appropriate style.

---

1   Ben, an English-speaking friend of yours who makes films for a TV company,
    has written to you. Read Ben's letter and the notes you have made. Then write a letter
    to Ben, using **all** your notes.

> *Guess what? My boss has asked me to make a short film for visitors to your town.*
>
> — **Great!**
>
> *I'll be in charge of a film crew of four so it'll be an interesting experience for me. We could come for one week either in January or August. When do you think would be better?*
>
> — **Say when and why**
>
> *In the film we'd like to show a place that's a bit unusual. Is there somewhere interesting that tourists don't normally visit?*
>
> — **Tell Ben**
>
> *Finally, we'll need someone to show us around the town. Do you know someone who might be able to help us?*
>
> — **Offer to help**
>
> *Please write back soon.*
>
> *Ben*

Write your **letter**. You must use grammatically correct sentences with accurate spelling and punctuation in a style appropriate for the situation.

Do not write any postal addresses.

Part 2

Write an answer to **one** of the questions **2–5** in this part. Write your answer in **120–180** words in an appropriate style.

---

2   You see this advertisement in an English language magazine.

> **GLOBAL MUSIC SHOPS**
> Rock Classical Pop Jazz
>
> We are looking for people to work in our international music shops for three months in the summer.
> ● Are you interested in music?
> ● Do you have any useful experience?
> ● Is your level of English good?
> Apply to the manager, Mr Boston, saying why you think you are suitable for the job in one of our music shops.

Write your **letter of application**. Do not write any postal addresses.

3   Your teacher has asked you to write a **story** for the school's English language magazine. The story must **begin** with the following words:

Tina was very excited when she heard that she had won the prize.

Write your **story**.

4   You see this announcement in an international travel magazine.

> **THE PERFECT HOLIDAY DESTINATION**
>
> Have you found the perfect holiday destination? If so, write us an **article**:
> ● describing the place
> ● saying why it is special for you.
> We will publish the best article next month.

Write your **article**.

5   Answer **one** of the following two questions based on **one** of the titles below.

(a) *The Citadel by* A. J. Cronin
'The character of Andrew Manson changes as we read The Citadel'.

Write an **essay**, saying whether you agree or disagree with this statement.

Write your **essay**.

(b) *Around the World in 80 Days* by Jules Verne
In *Around the World in 80 Days*, Passepartout makes a number of mistakes which delay Phileas Fogg's journey.

Write an **essay** describing one of these mistakes and say how Phileas deals with it.

Write your **essay**.

PAPER 3   USE OF ENGLISH (45 minutes)

Part 1

For questions **1–12**, read the text below and decide which answer (**A, B, C** or **D**) best fits each gap. There is an example at the beginning (**0**).

Mark your answers **on the separate answer sheet.**

Example:

0   **A** advantage   **B** benefit   **C** profit   **D** gain

THE PERFORMING ARTS

In the past, British children were frequently encouraged to try out their performing skills for the **(0)** ..... of adults. They did this by reading aloud, acting or **(1)** ..... a musical instrument. As they **(2)** ..... up they were taken to public places of entertainment – the theatre, opera, circus or ballet. They looked forward to these **(3)** ..... with great **(4)** ..... and would remember and discuss what they had seen for many weeks afterwards. But nowadays television and computers **(5)** ..... an endless stream of easily **(6)** ..... entertainment, and children quickly accept these marvellous **(7)** ..... as a very ordinary part of their everyday lives. For many children, the sense of witnessing a very **(8)** ..... live performance is gone forever.

But all is not lost. The **(9)** ..... of a TV set may have encouraged a very lazy response from **(10)** ..... in their own homes, but the **(11)** ..... of those with ambitions to become performing artists themselves does not seem to have been at all diminished. And live performances in public are still relatively **(12)** ....., albeit with an older, more specialist audience.

1	**A** controlling	**B** handling	**C** doing	**D** playing
2	**A** developed	**B** grew	**C** advanced	**D** brought
3	**A** circumstances	**B** occasions	**C** incidents	**D** situations
4	**A** sensation	**B** action	**C** thrill	**D** excitement
5	**A** supply	**B** send	**C** stock	**D** store
6	**A** applicable	**B** convenient	**C** available	**D** free
7	**A** designs	**B** inventions	**C** exhibits	**D** appearances
8	**A** special	**B** peculiar	**C** specific	**D** particular
9	**A** attendance	**B** presence	**C** being	**D** company
10	**A** spectators	**B** onlookers	**C** viewers	**D** listeners
11	**A** want	**B** appeal	**C** pressure	**D** desire
12	**A** famous	**B** favourite	**C** popular	**D** approved

Part 2

For questions **13–24**, read the text below and think of the word which best fits each gap. Use only **one** word in each gap. There is an example at the beginning **(0)**.

Write your answers **IN CAPITAL LETTERS on the separate answer sheet**.

Example: | 0 | O | N | E | | | | | | | | | | | | | | | | |

SWIMMING

Swimming is generally considered to be **(0)** ....*one*.... of the best ways of exercising the whole body without risk of injury. According to health experts, it can also ease back pain and even reduce blood pressure. There is only one problem: to enjoy all the benefits of swimming, you **(13)** .... to do it properly. **(14)** .... you visited your local swimming pool and just watched, you might be surprised to see **(15)** .... badly many people swim. Poor technique may result from a number of factors including anxiety, the swimmer's lack **(16)** .... body awareness, or just a concern about **(17)** .... their hair wet. What's **(18)** ...., swimming techniques do not always improve with practice. **(19)** .... the contrary, once people have fallen **(20)** .... bad habits, they tend to be stuck with them.

But help is at hand. For all those keen to learn to swim properly, and so **(21)** .... advantage of all the health benefits, there is now something known as the Shaw Method, developed by a former competitive swimmer, Steven Shaw. Shaw encourages people to think about their swimming technique and to concentrate on things **(22)** .... breathing correctly and making **(23)** .... that arm and leg movements work together **(24)** .... than against each other.

Part 3

For questions **25–34**, read the text below. Use the word given in capitals at the end of some of the lines to form a word that fits in the gap **in the same line**. There is an example at the beginning (**0**).

Write your answers **IN CAPITAL LETTERS on the separate answer sheet**.

Example:

AUSTRALIA

For years, Australia has had an (**0**) ....*irregular*.... pattern of population   **REGULAR**

distribution, with more people living in towns and cities in (**25**) ....   **COAST**

areas, especially the east and south-east, than in the interior of the

country. Since the 1940s, the population has become still more

(**26**) .... distributed with a significant rise in the number of people   **EVENLY**

living in these cities.

Cities are now the (**27**) .... centres of the country. An important   **ECONOMY**

element in their (**28**) .... has been the number of people from Europe   **GROW**

and Asia emigrating to Australia, especially in the second half of the

twentieth century. The new (**29**) .... decided to stay in the cities   **ARRIVE**

because (**30**) .... was easy to find there. Today, the population of   **EMPLOY**

Australia includes people who originally came from over 150 countries.

At one time, what made the (**31**) .... of people in Australia's cities so   **CONCENTRATE**

(**32**) .... was the country's dependence on the export of agricultural   **REMARK**

produce – indeed, the country's economy was founded on the production of

wheat and wool. This has since changed, not only with increased (**33**) ....   **INDUSTRY**

activity, but also with the rapid (**34**) .... of tourist and recreational   **EXPAND**

facilities. Tourism is now Australia's largest export industry.

Part 4

For questions **35–42**, complete the second sentence so that it has a similar meaning to the first sentence, using the word given. **Do not change the word given.** You must use between **two** and **five** words, including the word given. Here is an example (**0**).

Example:

0   You must do exactly what the manager tells you.

   CARRY

   You must .... instructions exactly.

The gap can be filled by the words 'carry out the manager's' so you write:

Example: | **0** | *CARRY OUT THE MANAGER'S* |

Write **only** the missing words **IN CAPITAL LETTERS on the separate answer sheet**.

---

35   I regret not contacting Brian when I was in Dublin.

   TOUCH

   I wish that I .... Brian when I was in Dublin.

36   In my opinion, these two kinds of music are completely different from each other.

   COMPARISON

   In my opinion, there is .... these two kinds of music.

37   I don't know why Sarah left the party so suddenly.

   MADE

   I don't know .... the party so suddenly.

38   Could you look after my cat while I'm away on holiday?

   CARE

   Would you mind .... my cat while I'm away on holiday?

39 We discussed the problem but nobody had a solution.

CAME

We discussed the problem but .... with a solution.

40 Claire was not allowed to stay out late when she lived at home with her parents.

LET

Claire's parents .... stay out late when she lived at home.

41 I arrived late because I missed the 10.30 train.

TURNED

If I'd caught the 10.30 train, I .... time.

42 Floods meant rescue workers could not get through to the village.

PREVENTED

Rescue workers .... through to the village by floods.

PAPER 4 LISTENING (approximately 40 minutes)

Part 1

You will hear people talking in eight different situations. For questions **1–8**, choose the best answer (**A**, **B** or **C**).

---

1   You hear some information about a country on a travel programme.
    Where do most people spend the summer months?

    A   at the seaside

    B   in the capital city

    C   in the mountains

2   You hear part of a radio programme about chewing gum.
    What is the speaker doing?

    A   outlining its history

    B   describing why it has changed

    C   explaining its popularity

3   You hear part of a radio programme where listeners phone in with their opinions.
    What does the man want to do?

    A   express his disappointment

    B   complain about his situation

    C   encourage other listeners

4   You hear a woman speaking on the radio about buying a painting for the first time.
    What opinion is she expressing?

    A   A painting can be a worthwhile investment.

    B   Only buy a painting if you have room for it.

    C   Take your time when buying your first painting.

5 You hear a man being interviewed on the radio.
What does he say about his mother?

    A   She helped him become an artist.

    B   She persuaded him to do research.

    C   She wanted him to make money.

6 You hear part of an interview with a woman who is talking about her day.
What is her profession?

    A   a teacher

    B   a doctor

    C   a farmer

7 You hear a man talking on the radio about teaching beginners to surf in the sea.
What does the man say about beginners?

    A   They are very sensitive to criticism.

    B   They need to be given appropriate goals.

    C   They often start off with the wrong attitude.

8 You hear part of an interview with a crime novelist.
What point is he making about his novels?

    A   They are based on real-life crimes.

    B   They include accurate descriptions of life in the past.

    C   They vary in length depending on the historical period.

Part 2

You will hear a man called Peter Welby, who makes small models of buildings, talking about his work. For questions **9–18**, complete the sentences.

The Model Maker

Before becoming a model maker, Peter did a course in

| | 9 | at a college.

Peter compares his job to the type of work done by a | | 10 |

In Peter's hardest job, he was given some

| | 11 | of the building to work from.

Peter's most enjoyable job was making a model of a

| | 12 | for an exhibition.

Most of Peter's work is exported to | *and* | 13 |

Peter says his models look best when they have

| | 14 | directed onto them.

Peter's model of Marney House measures | | 15 | in height.

The Marney House model took a long time to make because it had so many

| | 16 | and roof tiles.

The roof tiles on the model of Marney House are made of | | 17 |

Peter uses watercolour paint to reproduce the effects of the weather and

| | 18 |

Part 3

You will hear five different people talking about hotels they have recently stayed in with their children. For questions **19–23**, choose from the list (**A–F**) what each speaker says. Use the letters only once. There is one extra letter which you do not need to use.

A Teenagers might not enjoy staying at this particular hotel.

| | Speaker 1 | | 19 |

B The hotel was quite expensive.

| | Speaker 2 | | 20 |

C A playground would have improved the facilities.

| | Speaker 3 | | 21 |

D The hotel needed to know if you wanted your children to eat early.

| | Speaker 4 | | 22 |

E There was no swimming pool available in the hotel.

| | Speaker 5 | | 23 |

F Children under ten were not allowed to stay at the hotel.

Part 4

You will hear a radio interview with a young tennis player, Alice Winters and her coach, Bruce Gray. For questions **24–30**, choose the best answer (**A**, **B** or **C**).

24 What does Bruce say about getting financial help?

    A   He is surprised by how hard it is to get any.

    B   He expects that they will get some soon.

    C   He thinks they can succeed without it.

25 What is Alice's attitude towards training?

    A   She enjoys organising it herself.

    B   She wishes she had more time for other things.

    C   She sometimes finds it hard to make the effort.

26 What is Alice's attitude towards her schoolwork?

    A   She is determined to do well in it.

    B   It is not the most important thing.

    C   She is confident of her ability.

27 How does Alice feel about competitions?

    A   The result is the most important thing.

    B   Losing weakens her confidence.

    C   She always expects to win.

28 According to Bruce, what makes Alice exceptional?

    A   her natural talent for the game

    B   the amount of effort she puts in

    C   the way she reacts to other players

29 How does Alice feel about becoming a professional player?

   A   She is looking forward to the glamorous lifestyle.

   B   She realises she may not be successful.

   C   She is worried about getting on with the other players.

30 How does Bruce describe Alice's character?

   A   She's a very sociable person.

   B   She tends to be rather moody.

   C   She is surprisingly mature.

PAPER 5   SPEAKING (14 minutes)

You take the Speaking test with another candidate, referred to here as your partner.
There are two examiners. One will speak to you and your partner and the other will be
listening. Both examiners will award marks.

Part 1 (3 minutes)

The examiner asks you and your partner questions about yourselves. You may be asked
about things like 'your home town', 'your interests', 'your career plans', etc.

Part 2 (a one-minute 'long turn' for each candidate, plus 20-second response from the second candidate)

The examiner gives you two photographs and asks you to talk about them for one
minute. The examiner then asks your partner a question about your photographs and
your partner responds briefly.

Then the examiner gives your partner two different photographs. Your partner talks
about these photographs for one minute. This time the examiner asks you a question
about your partner's photographs and you respond briefly.

Part 3 (approximately 3 minutes)

The examiner asks you and your partner to talk together. You may be asked to solve a
problem or try to come to a decision about something. For example, you might be asked
to decide the best way to use some rooms in a language school. The examiner gives
you a picture to help you but does not join in the conversation.

Part 4 (approximately 4 minutes)

The interlocutor asks some further questions, which leads to a more general discussion
of what you have talked about in Part 3. You may comment on your partner's answers
if you wish.

Test 4

PAPER 1   READING (1 hour)

Part 1

You are going to read an extract from a short story. For questions **1–8**, choose the answer (**A**, **B**, **C** or **D**) which you think fits best according to the text.

Mark your answers **on the separate answer sheet**.

We always went to Ireland in June. Ever since the four of us began to go on holidays together we had spent the first fortnight of the month at Glencorn Lodge in County Antrim. It's a large house by the sea, not far from the village of Ardbeag. The English couple who bought the house, the Malseeds, have had to add to the building, but everything has been done most discreetly.

It was Strafe who found Glencorn for us. He'd come across an advertisement in the days when the Malseeds still felt the need to advertise. 'How about this?' he said one evening and read out the details. We had gone away together the summer before, to a hotel that had been recommended by friends, but it hadn't been a success because the food was so appalling.

The four of us have been playing cards together for ages, Dekko, Strafe, Cynthia and myself. They call me Milly, though strictly speaking my name is Dorothy Milson. Dekko picked up his nickname at school, Dekko Deacon sounding rather good, I suppose. He and Strafe were at school together, which must be why we call Strafe by his surname as the teachers used to. We're all about the same age and live quite close to the town where the Malseeds were before they decided to make the change from England to Ireland. Quite a coincidence, we always think.

'How very nice,' Mrs Malseed said, smiling her welcome again this year. Some instinct seems to tell her when guests are about to arrive, for she's rarely not waiting in the large, low-ceilinged hall that always smells of flowers. 'Arthur, take the luggage up,' she commanded the old porter. 'Rose, Tulip, Lily and Geranium.' She referred to the names of the rooms reserved for us. Mrs Malseed herself painted flowers on the doors of the hotel instead of putting numbers. In winter, when no one much comes to Glencorn Lodge, she sees to little details like that; her husband sees to redecoration and repairs.

'Well, well, well,' Mr Malseed said, now entering the hall through the door that leads to the kitchen. 'A hundred thousand welcomes,' he greeted us in the Irish manner. He was smiling broadly with his dark brown eyes twinkling, making us think we were rather more than just another group of hotel guests. Everyone smiled, and I could feel the others thinking that our holiday had truly begun. Nothing had changed at Glencorn, all was well. Kitty from the dining room came out to greet us. 'You look younger every year, all four of you,' she said, causing everyone in the hall to laugh again. Arthur led the way to the rooms, carrying as much of our luggage as he could manage and returning for the remainder.

After dinner we played cards for a while but not going on for as long as we might because we were still quite tired after the journey. In the lounge there was a man on his own and a French couple. There had been other people at dinner, of course, because in June Glencorn Lodge is always full: from where we sat in the window we could see some of them strolling about the lawns, others taking the cliff path down to the seashore. In the morning we'd do the same: we'd walk along the sands to Ardbeag and have coffee in the hotel there, back in time for lunch. In the afternoon we'd drive somewhere.

I knew all that because over the years this kind of pattern had developed. Since first we came here, we'd all fallen hopelessly in love with every variation of its remarkable landscape.

1   Why did the Malseeds no longer advertise Glencorn Lodge?

    A It was too expensive.
    B It was not necessary.
    C It was too complicated.
    D It was not effective.

2   What did Dekko and the writer have in common?

    A They did not like their names.
    B People used their surnames when speaking to them.
    C They chose their own nicknames.
    D People did not call them by their real names.

3   The coincidence referred to in paragraph three is that the four friends and the Malseeds

    A came from the same area.
    B preferred Ireland to England.
    C lived close to one another.
    D were all about the same age.

4   What was special about the rooms at Glencorn Lodge?

    A They had been painted by Mrs Malseed herself.
    B There was no paint on the doors.
    C They did not have numbers.
    D There were different flowers in all of them.

5   What did the writer particularly like about Mr Malseed?

    A He had nice brown eyes.
    B He always came to welcome them.
    C He made guests feel like friends.
    D He spoke in the Irish way.

6   Why did the writer feel contented after Mr Malseed had spoken?

    A Everything was as it had always been.
    B The holiday would start at any moment.
    C A few things had improved at Glencorn.
    D Her friends had enjoyed the holiday.

7   What did Kitty do which made the friends laugh?

    A She told them a joke.
    B She pretended to insult them.
    C She laughed when she saw them.
    D She paid them a compliment.

8   The next day the friends would walk to Ardbeag because

    A they would be able to walk on the sands.
    B this was what they always did.
    C they wanted to do the same as other people.
    D it was quite a short walk for them.

Part 2

You are going to read a newspaper article about people who make films about wild animals in Africa. Seven sentences have been removed from the article. Choose from the sentences **A–H** the one which fits each gap (**9–15**). There is one extra sentence which you do not need to use.

Mark your answers **on the separate answer sheet**.

IN THEIR NATURAL HABITAT

What keeps film-makers Amanda Barrett and Owen Newman away from their home comforts for months on end? The search for the perfect shot.

Of all the creatures to be found in the jungles and plains of East Africa, two of the hardest to track down must surely be producer Amanda Barrett and cameraman Owen Newman.

Their present habitat, the Ngorongoro Crater, has been lashed by six months of almost continuous rain, giving rise to a number of unforeseen problems. **9** His working partnership with the talented producer has created some of TV's finest wildlife films, such as their amazing and well-received film on leopards.

10 But this is nothing unusual in television partnerships. Travelling film-makers have been constantly circling the globe, in order to point cameras at exotic wildlife ever since the birth of television.

I spoke to Newman about their partnership while he was making one of his rare and unpredictable reunions with other members of the human race at a safari lodge. 'We do have occasional arguments but we tend to get over them fairly quickly,' he says of his colleague. **11**

'When we are on the move, we have to put up our tents each night. But this time we are operating much more of a fixed camp, and as we set out at 5 a.m. each morning, we tend to make the tea the night before and keep it warm in a vacuum flask.'

12 'It's not unusual for us to be out and about for up to eight weeks at a time, so catering does cause the odd panic,' says Newman.

13 'I remember once we were filming a family of lions and there was one lioness who would regularly go off on her own. Whenever she returned, she would go round and greet all the other members of the pride, and after a while she made a point of greeting our car as part of her round.'

It was back in 1988 that Newman first worked with Barrett on a film called 'The Great Rift', and two more years before they set off as a team to film Arctic foxes. **14** And before they get the green light, they have to submit a script for approval.

'Amanda and I struck up a good working relationship from the start,' says Newman, 'because it was obvious that we shared the same ideas and overall vision. **15** I believe if you can evoke an emotional response from people, that is far better than if you appeal only to their heads.'

A Even while this film of one of Africa's shyest cats was being shown, the pair were already back where they belong – this time trailing that equally shy animal, the jackal.

B It can be a rough existence, but the appeal of being alone in such remote areas is that we can get close enough to the animals to become part of their lives.

C Neither of them regard themselves as the leader, and he says that one of the reasons why they get on so well with each other is that they both see the animals in a similar way.

D Since then, they have learned to set aside four months on location to gather sufficient material for each half-hour film.

E In Africa, however, they are seldom sighted at all as they scour the vast Serengeti Plain, their two vehicles packed with cameras, drinking water, camping gear and food.

F The rest of the Newman–Barrett daily diet consists of pre-packed meals heated and dished out by whoever is at hand at the time.

G What we are always seeking to achieve is a film that is rich in atmosphere, that brings to life the true spirit of the place and animals, and that will touch people's hearts.

H Newman explained that they had to invest in an expensive piece of equipment so that whenever one of their vehicles gets stuck in the mud, Amanda can pull him back to safety.

Part 3

You are going to read an article about three pairs of women who exchanged jobs for a day. For questions **16–30**, choose from the women (**A–F**). The women may be chosen more than once.

Mark your answers **on the separate answer sheet.**

Which woman says she

thought about the person she changed places with?	**16**
found the routine much busier than in her normal job?	**17**
discovered she wasn't very good at the job she tried?	**18**
found the work she did for one day worthwhile?	**19**
found some of the people she came across hard to handle?	**20**
had difficulty making a decision?	**21**
didn't enjoy being the centre of attention?	**22**
appreciated the relationships among her new colleagues?	**23**
thought the clothes she wore gained her more respect?	**24**
was surprised at her own reaction to some aspects of the job she tried?	**25**
might consider doing similar work to the job she tried?	**26**
doesn't normally deal with people on an individual basis?	**27**
had not had a realistic idea of the job before she tried it for a day?	**28**
was given some information which she was already aware of?	**29**
noticed the problems of the other people she was working with?	**30**

Changing Lives with a Stranger

What would it be like to live somebody else's life for a day?

A Mandie Currie, a zoo-keeper, spent the day in the offices of the magazine Marie Claire.

'Choosing what to wear for my day at Marie Claire was tricky because normally I wear a uniform at work. First I went to a still-life photo studio, then to press previews, all before lunch. The zoo is such a tranquil, peaceful place – and here I was rushing around when I could be sitting quietly giving an animal a cuddle. Some of the members of the fashion team seemed quite stressed – my job doesn't really get pressurised. At a fashion shoot in the afternoon, it made me laugh to think that I'd usually be cleaning out cages or handling rats. I'm fascinated to see how magazines work, but I really enjoy my job at the zoo so I'll stay put.'

B Alice Cutler, a fashion assistant at Marie Claire, spent the day at London Zoo.

'I arrived at the zoo in my leather boots and dark blue trousers. The zoo gave me a green polo shirt instead to work in – which was just as well, as I got very dirty. As I stroked one of the elephants, I reckoned Mandie would probably be packing up clothes in the cupboard. By five o'clock, I stank but I'd had such a brilliant day. When I retire from fashion, I could see myself working with elephants – but maybe in Africa.'

C Karen Hodson, a nurse at Hammersmith Hospital, went on location with the television gardening programme Ground Force.

'I was extremely excited about meeting the team, and Alan Titchmarsh, the programme presenter, was really nice. One of the things I liked was the chance to be in the fresh air. Depending on my shifts, I sometimes never see daylight. Even though it was hard work, it was great fun. I thought I was pretty strong but I felt weak compared with the rest of the team. My romantic vision of landscape gardening had not included physical hard work or meticulous planning. I was more an enthusiastic than effective gardener, so I don't plan to give up my other job.'

D Charlie Dimmock, landscape gardener with the TV programme Ground Force, worked a shift at Hammersmith Hospital.

'I made beds and handed out tablets. I expected to faint when I was doing some jobs, but I amazed myself by finding that it didn't bother me. The friendship among the nurses is great, and it felt tremendously 'girlie' compared with my normal male environment. I feel my job is a real waste of time compared with nursing. My day at the hospital was not exactly pleasant but it left me with a great sense of satisfaction.'

E Lucy Harvey, a personal trainer, spent the day with the airline Ryanair as a member of the cabin crew.

'I changed into the uniform, and the moment I put it on I felt completely different – people suddenly look up to you. Before the flight, our supervisor told us about safety, what to do if someone had a heart attack – which I knew about from my fitness training. When the passengers boarded the flight to Paris I gave out magazines. Everyone stared at me and I felt very self-conscious. On the return journey, we had 80 schoolchildren on board who wouldn't sit still. I wished I was back in the gym with one sensible adult to look after.'

F Sonia McDermott, an air hostess with the airline Ryanair, spent the day as a personal trainer in a gym.

'I was dreading doing this swap as I don't do any exercise. I was amazed at how much attention you give to one person. In my job you meet 130 passengers four times a day. I was very surprised at lunch to see that some of the trainers didn't eat ultra-healthily, but they all drink lots of water. I wouldn't swap my job for this. However, it has inspired me to join a gym and try to be a bit healthier.'

PAPER 2   WRITING (1 hour 20 minutes)

Part 1

You **must** answer this question. Write your answer in **120–150** words in an appropriate style.

1   You recently received an email from your English-speaking friend, Pat, inviting you to stay and asking you to a special party. Read Pat's email and the notes you have made. Then write an email to Pat, using **all** your notes.

---

email

From:	Pat
Sent:	10th July
Subject:	Invitation

You said you'd like to come and stay for a while in the summer, so I'm writing to ask if you'd like to visit in July.

July perfect because…

By the way, it's my brother Tim's 18th birthday on 10th July, so try to be here then, because there'll be a big special party to go to. Lots of our friends and relatives will be there!

Birthday present – tell Pat my ideas

I'm on holiday in July too, so perhaps we could go camping for a few days as well?

No, because…

If you're coming, let me know if there's anything else you'd particularly like to do. Then I can make some plans.

Yes – could we …

Write soon, won't you?

Pat

Write your **email**. You must use grammatically correct sentences with accurate spelling and punctuation in a style appropriate for the situation.

Visual materials for the Speaking test

• What are the advantages and disadvantages of living in the different places?

1A

1B

- Why would people keep these photographs?
- Which photograph is the most special?

1E

• Why is it important to ask questions in these situations?

1C

1D

- Why do people enjoy activities like these in their free time?

2A

2B

- How can these things help people to enjoy life in a city?
- Which two things are the most important?

2E

• Why do people choose to shop in places like these?

2C

2D

• What are the people enjoying about spending time by these rivers?

3A

3B

- How would these ideas help people to get to know each other?
- Which idea would be the most successful?

3E

• What is difficult about preparing meals in these situations?

3C

3D

• Why do people choose to go to beaches like these?

4A

4B

- What are the advantages and disadvantages of the different jobs?
- Which job would be the most interesting to do for a short time?

4E

• What can be difficult about doing these things?

4C

4D

Part 2

Write an answer to **one** of the questions **2–5** in this part. Write your answer in **120–180** words in an appropriate style.

2   You have had a class discussion on the environment. Your teacher has now asked you to write an **essay**, giving your opinion on the following statement:

We must look after the world – it is our home.

Write your **essay**.

3   You see this announcement in an international travel magazine.

> # PLANE, TRAIN OR BOAT?
> Which is **YOUR** favourite way to travel, and why?
> Write us an **article** telling us which one you prefer.
> The best article will be published and the winner will receive £200.

Write your **article**.

4   An international organisation wants to hold a festival in your region to promote food from around the world. You have been asked to write a **report** about the food specialities in your region, where local people enjoy going out to eat and in what ways you think people's eating habits have changed in the last ten years.

Write your **report**.

5   Answer **one** of the following two questions based on **one** of the titles below.

(a)   *The Citadel* by A. J. Cronin

This is part of a letter from your English-speaking penfriend:
There are some really unpleasant characters in The Citadel, aren't there? Out of all of them, who did you dislike the most?

Write a **letter** to your penfriend, giving your opinion. Do not write any postal addresses.

Write your **letter**.

(b)   *Around the World in 80 Days* by Jules Verne
Apart from Passepartout, Phileas Fogg is accompanied on his journey in *Around the World in 80 Days* by Mrs Aouda and Mr Fix.

Write an **essay** saying which character adds more to the story and why.

Write your **essay**.

PAPER 3 USE OF ENGLISH (45 minutes)

Part 1

For questions **1–12**, read the text below and decide which answer (**A, B, C** or **D**) best fits each gap. There is an example at the beginning (**0**).

Mark your answers **on the separate answer sheet.**

Example:

0 **A** consider   **B** know   **C** call   **D** label

0	A	B	C	D
	—	—	▬	—

SHOPPING MALLS

Victor Gruen, an American architect, revolutionised shopping in the 1950s by creating the type of shopping centre that we now **(0)** ..... a shopping mall.

Gruen's **(1)** ..... was to provide a pleasant, quiet and spacious shopping environment with large car parks, which usually **(2)** ..... building in the suburbs. He also wanted people to be able to shop in all kinds of weather. He **(3)** ..... on using building designs that he knew people would feel **(4)** ..... with, but placed them in landscaped 'streets' that were entirely enclosed and often covered with a curved glass roof. This was done to **(5)** ..... some of the older shopping arcades of city centres, but while these housed only small speciality shops, Gruen's shopping malls were on a much grander **(6)** ..... .

Access to the whole shopping mall was gained by using the main doors, which **(7)** ..... the shopping 'streets' from the parking **(8)** ..... outside. As there was no need to **(9)** ..... out bad weather, shops no longer needed windows and doors, and people could wander **(10)** ..... from shop to shop. In many cities, shopping malls now **(11)** ..... much more than just shops; cinemas, restaurants and other forms of entertainment are also **(12)** ..... in popularity.

1 **A** direction   **B** aim   **C** search   **D** view

2 **A** resulted   **B** sought   **C** intended   **D** meant

3 **A** insisted   **B** demanded   **C** requested   **D** emphasised

4 **A** favourable   **B** agreeable   **C** comfortable **D** enviable

5 **A** model   **B** imitate   **C** repeat   **D** shadow

6 **A** measure   **B** height   **C** size   **D** scale

7 **A** disconnected   **B** withdrew   **C** separated   **D** parted

8 **A** strips   **B** lines   **C** areas   **D** plots

9 **A** hold   **B** get   **C** stay   **D** keep

10 **A** freely   **B** loosely   **C** simply   **D** entirely

11 **A** contain   **B** concern   **C** consist   **D** compose

12 **A** becoming   **B** growing   **C** raising   **D** advancing

Part 2

For questions **13–24**, read the text below and think of the word which best fits each gap. Use only **one** word in each gap. There is an example at the beginning (**0**).

Write your answers **IN CAPITAL LETTERS on the separate answer sheet**.

Example: | 0 | T | H | E | | | | | | | | | | | | | | | |

SUMMER CAMP

Every year, eight million children across ....*the*.... United States spend some time at a summer camp. For more than a century, children **(13)** .... enjoyed both learning new skills and **(14)** .... part in a variety of activities in a friendly environment.

There are 10,000 camps across the country, **(15)** .... are designed to look **(16)** .... youngsters from the age of six to eighteen. The camps, lasting anything from one to eight weeks, are often situated in beautiful lakeside areas and there is **(17)** .... wide range of prices to suit every pocket. The children typically do outdoor activities, including some challenging sports like climbing, or indoor activities **(18)** .... as drama, music or poetry.

(19) .... the camps are not luxurious, the wooden cabins the young people sleep in are comfortable. The timetable does not allow very **(20)** .... time for relaxing because the children **(21)** .... kept busy all the time. The camps are popular with the children, and many come away **(22)** .... of enthusiasm. In the words of one former camper, 'I made a lot of friends, **(23)** .... never on my own, and became a lot **(24)** .... self-confident.'

Part 3

For questions **25–34**, read the text below. Use the word given in capitals at the end of some of the lines to form a word that fits in the gap **in the same line**. There is an example at the beginning (**0**).

Write your answers **IN CAPITAL LETTERS on the separate answer sheet**.

Example: | 0 | S | C | I | E | N | T | I | S | T | S | | | | | | | |

REMEMBERING YOUR DREAMS

A team of **(0)** ....*scientists*...., who have studied the subject of · · · · · · · · · · **SCIENCE**
dreams, have come up with some interesting conclusions. First
of all, everybody, without exception, has them. Secondly, dreams
can be of practical value, acting as a **(25)** .... of things of · · · · · · · **REMIND**
(26) .... that we need to do in our waking lives. If you dream · · · **IMPORTANT**
of the punishment you may receive for not handing in your homework
(27) .... , for example, this may help you to do it on time. Indeed, · · · **PUNCTUAL**
things we are **(28)** .... about in our daily lives often feature in · · · **ANXIETY**
our dreams.

But it is hard to make sense of your dreams if you lack the **(29)** .... · · · **ABLE**
to remember them in the first place. One **(30)** .... is that you should · · **RECOMMEND**
keep a diary and pen by your bed, so you can write down your dreams
as soon as they occur. You should concentrate on three aspects. Firstly,
record the strongest emotion in your dream, whether it is fear, **(31)** .... · · **ANGRY**
or whatever. Then write down anything strange or **(32)** .... that · · · **USUAL**
happened and the names of the people who made an **(33)** .... in your · · **APPEAR**
dream. This way, according to the experts, you will have a **(34)** .... and · · **RELY**
meaningful dream record, which will make for fascinating reading.

Part 4

For questions **35–42**, complete the second sentence so that it has a similar meaning to the first sentence, using the word given. **Do not change the word given**. You must use between **two** and **five** words, including the word given. Here is an example (**0**).

Example:

0   You must do exactly what the manager tells you.

CARRY

You must .... instructions exactly.

The gap can be filled by the words 'carry out the manager's' so you write:

Example: | **0** | *CARRY OUT THE MANAGER'S* |

Write **only** the missing words **IN CAPITAL LETTERS on the separate answer sheet**.

---

35   Today's meeting is postponed and it will be held next week.

PUT

Today's meeting has .... until next week.

36   According to the report, the driver of the car was a policeman.

BEING

According to the report, the .... by a policeman.

37   Nobody spoke for about five minutes.

BEFORE

It was about five minutes .... anything.

38   Mr Johnson continued to get up at 6.30 even after he retired.

CARRIED

Mr Johnson .... at 6.30 even after he retired.

39 I prefer eating sandwiches to a cooked lunch.

RATHER

I .... sandwiches than a cooked lunch.

40 'I'm sorry I behaved so badly,' said George.

APOLOGISED

George .... so badly.

41 There's no chance of Jenny getting here on time.

POSSIBLE

It won't be .... here on time.

42 'We really don't need to leave early,' said Elena.

POINT

'There's really .... early,' said Elena.

PAPER 4   LISTENING (approximately 40 minutes)

Part 1

You will hear people talking in eight different situations. For questions **1–8**, choose the best answer (**A**, **B** or **C**).

---

1   You hear someone talking about women's football.
        What is she doing when she speaks?

    A   encouraging young girls to support a team

    B   suggesting how to attract young girls to the sport

    C   asking young girls to take the sport seriously

2   You hear a man talking on the radio about a bag made for use on walking trips.
        How does this new bag differ from others?

    A   It has pockets on the side.

    B   You can take off the rain cover.

    C   There are some extra features.

3   On the radio, you hear a man discussing a cartoon film about dinosaurs.
        What aspect of the film disappointed him?

    A   the design of the backgrounds

    B   the quality of the sound effects

    C   the size of the dinosaurs

4   You overhear a couple talking about keeping fit.
        What do they agree about?

    A   the need to be more active

    B   the benefits of joining a gym

    C   the dangers of too much exercise

5 In a radio play, you hear a woman talking on the phone to a friend.
Where does the woman want her friend to meet her?

A on the beach

B at the bank

C in a shop

6 You hear a student talking to his friend about a meeting with his tutor.
What was the student's purpose in meeting his tutor?

A to see if there was a part-time job available

B to ask for financial assistance

C to request more time to complete coursework

7 You hear a man talking about learning how to paint landscapes.
What does he say about it?

A It proved easier than he had thought.

B It showed him he had some talent.

C It opened up opportunities for him.

8 You turn on the radio and hear a man talking.
What is he talking about?

A finding friendship

B solving problems

C helping others

Part 2

You will hear an interview with a man called Richard Porter who is a maker of musical instruments called organs. For questions **9–18**, complete the sentences.

Musical Instrument Maker

Richard's first ambition was to be a [_____ **9**]

Richard makes organs which are used in [_____ **10**] and churches worldwide.

It costs £ [_____ **11**] to buy one of the organs which Richard makes.

According to Richard, personal [_____ **12**] provide him with most of his overseas clients.

Richard says that he is involved in [_____ **13**] organs, as well as building and selling them.

In terms of raw materials, only the [_____ **14**] that Richard uses comes from Britain.

Richard's new workshop will be in a building that was once used as a [_____ **15**]

Richard will have to work in a [_____ **16**] as well as in his new workshop.

The only thing that Richard will have to pay for in his new workshop is the [_____ **17**]

The new workshop will be perfect for the instruments Richard makes because it is a [_____ **18**] place.

Part 3

You will hear five different cyclists talking about a long-distance race they took part in. For questions **19–23**, choose from the list (**A–F**) what each speaker says. Use the letters only once. There is one extra letter which you do not need to use.

A I started the race but then decided not to continue.

Speaker 1		19

B I had to change bicycles during the race.

Speaker 2		20

C I felt uncomfortable on my bicycle throughout the race.

Speaker 3		21

D I had done some serious physical training for the race.

Speaker 4		22

E I think the organisers of the race were inefficient.

Speaker 5		23

F I was satisfied with my performance in the race.

Part 4

You will hear an interview with a TV presenter, Tanya Edwards, who is talking about her career and her daughter called Maddy. For questions **24–30**, choose the best answer (**A**, **B** or **C**).

24 What does Tanya say about her first job in children's TV?

    A   She had contacted the TV company earlier.

    B   It was difficult to get used to the instructions.

    C   Her previous experience was useful.

25 What does Tanya say about Paul Broadly, her first boss?

    A   He thought of nothing but his work.

    B   It was difficult to work with him.

    C   He was unwilling to share ideas about the work.

26 What does Tanya say about her parachute jump?

    A   She wishes she had never done it.

    B   It resulted in unexpected attention.

    C   Her boss was cross about what happened.

27 What does Tanya say about her daughter's flute playing?

    A   She knew that Maddy had talent.

    B   She saw that Maddy liked an audience.

    C   She wanted Maddy to practise more.

28 How does Tanya feel when her daughter sings in public?

    A   responsible for Maddy's success

    B   worried that something will go wrong

    C   aware of how the audience feels

29 Tanya says that Maddy finds modelling difficult because

   A   she finds it exhausting.

   B   you have to cope with criticism.

   C   people don't respect models.

30 What is Tanya's attitude to fame in general?

   A   You should enjoy it while it lasts.

   B   You should try and ignore it.

   C   You should accept its drawbacks.

PAPER 5 SPEAKING (14 minutes)

You take the Speaking test with another candidate, referred to here as your partner. There are two examiners. One will speak to you and your partner and the other will be listening. Both examiners will award marks.

Part 1 (3 minutes)

The examiner asks you and your partner questions about yourselves. You may be asked about things like 'your home town', 'your interests', 'your career plans', etc.

Part 2 (a one-minute 'long turn' for each candidate, plus 20-second response from the second candidate)

The examiner gives you two photographs and asks you to talk about them for one minute. The examiner then asks your partner a question about your photographs and your partner responds briefly.

Then the examiner gives your partner two different photographs. Your partner talks about these photographs for one minute. This time the examiner asks you a question about your partner's photographs and you respond briefly.

Part 3 (approximately 3 minutes)

The examiner asks you and your partner to talk together. You may be asked to solve a problem or try to come to a decision about something. For example, you might be asked to decide the best way to use some rooms in a language school. The examiner gives you a picture to help you but does not join in the conversation.

Part 4 (approximately 4 minutes)

The interlocutor asks some further questions, which leads to a more general discussion of what you have talked about in Part 3. You may comment on your partner's answers if you wish.

Paper 5 frames

Test 1

Note: In the examination, there will be both an assessor and an interlocutor in the room.
   The visual material for **Test 1** appears on pages C1 and C4 (Part 2), and C2–C3 (Part 3).

Part 1   3 minutes (5 minutes for groups of three)

Interlocutor: Good morning/afternoon/evening. My name is ………… and this is my
                   colleague ………… .
                   And your names are?
                   Can I have your mark sheets, please?
                   Thank you.
                   First of all, we'd like to know something about you.

- Where are you from *(Candidate A)*?
- And you *(Candidate B)*?
- What do you like about living *(here / name of candidate's home town)*?
- And what about you *(Candidate A/B)*?

Select one or more questions from any of the following categories, as appropriate.

Leisure time

- Do you spend most of your free time on your own or with friends? (What do
  you usually do?)
- Do you prefer to be outside or inside when you have free time? (Why?)

Likes and dislikes

- What is your favourite part of the day? (Why?)
- Do you enjoy shopping? (What sort of things do you <u>not</u> enjoy buying?)

Science and technology

- How much do you use the Internet? (What do you use it for?)
- Do you enjoy playing computer games? (Why? / Why not?)

Part 2   4 minutes (6 minutes for groups of three)

Places to live
Asking questions

Interlocutor: In this part of the test, I'm going to give each of you two photographs.
                   I'd like you to talk about your photographs on your own for about a minute,
                   and also to answer a short question about your partner's photographs.

> (*Candidate A*), it's your turn first. Here are your photographs. They show different places where people live.
>
> *Indicate pictures 1A and 1B on page C1 to Candidate A.*
>
> I'd like you to compare the photographs, and say what are the advantages and disadvantages of living in different places. All right?

Candidate A: [*1 minute.*]

Interlocutor: Thank you.
(*Candidate B*), would you like to live near the sea?

Candidate B: [*Approximately 20 seconds.*]

Interlocutor: Thank you.

> Now, (*Candidate B*), here are your two photographs. They show people asking questions in different situations.
>
> *Indicate pictures 1C and 1D on page C4 to Candidate B.*
>
> I'd like you to compare the photographs, and say why you think it's important to ask questions in these situations. All right?

Candidate B: [*1 minute.*]

Interlocutor: Thank you.
(*Candidate A*), would you like to work as a teacher?

Candidate A: [*Approximately 20 seconds.*]

Interlocutor: Thank you.

Parts 3 and 4   7 minutes (9 minutes for groups of three)

Part 3

Special photographs

Interlocutor: Now, I'd like you to talk about something together for about three minutes. (*4 minutes for groups of three.*)

> People often keep photographs to remind themselves of special times in their lives. Here are some pictures that people have decided to keep.
>
> *Indicate the set of pictures 1E on pages C2–C3 to the candidates.*
>
> First, talk to each other about why you think people would keep these photographs. Then decide which photograph you think is the most special. All right?

Candidates: [*3 minutes.*]

Interlocutor: Thank you.

Part 4

Interlocutor: *Select any of the following questions as*
                  appropriate:

Select any of the following
prompts as appropriate:
• What do you think?
• Do you agree?
• And you?

- What sort of photographs do you like to keep?
- Do you like it when people take photographs of you? Why? / Why not?
- Why do you think some people are so interested in looking at photographs of famous people?
- What is the best way to remember places you've visited taking: photographs or buying souvenirs? Why?
- Do you think it's a good idea to always take a camera with you on holiday? Why? / Why not?
- Is it a good idea to keep a diary to help you remember special times? Why?

Thank you. That is the end of the test.

TEST 2

Note: In the examination, there will be both an assessor and an interlocutor in the room.
The visual material for **Test 2** appears on pages C5 and C8 (Part 2), and C6–C7 (Part 3).

Part 1   3 minutes (5 minutes for groups of three)

Interlocutor: Good morning/afternoon/evening. My name is .... and this is my colleague ....
And your names are?
Can I have your mark sheets, please?
Thank you.
First of all, we'd like to know something about you.

- Where are you from *(Candidate A)*?
- And you *(Candidate B)*?
- What do you like about living *(here / name of candidate's home town)*?
- And what about you *(Candidate A/B)*?

Select one or more questions from any of the following categories, as appropriate.

Likes and dislikes

- What kind of music do you listen to? (When do you listen to music?)
- Do you enjoy watching films? (Tell us about a film you've enjoyed recently.)

Work and education

- Do you think you will use English a lot in the future? (In what ways?)
- What other languages would you like to learn? (Why?)

Travel and holidays

- What is your favourite place for a holiday? (Why?)
- What do you enjoy doing on holiday?

Part 2   4 minutes (6 minutes for groups of three)

Free time
Places to shop

Interlocutor: In this part of the test, I'm going to give each of you two photographs. I'd like you to talk about your photographs on your own for about a minute, and also to answer a short question about your partner's photographs.

(Candidate A), it's your turn first. Here are your photographs. They show people enjoying their free time in different ways.

Indicate pictures 2A and 2B on page C5 to Candidate A.

I'd like you to compare the photographs, and say why you think people enjoy activities like these in their free time. All right?

Candidate A:	[*1 minute.*]
Interlocutor:	Thank you. *(Candidate B)*, have you ever been ice skating?
Candidate B:	[*Approximately 20 seconds.*]
Interlocutor:	Thank you.

Now, *(Candidate B)*, here are your two photographs. They show people buying and selling different things.

Indicate pictures 2C and 2D on page C8 to Candidate B.

I'd like you to compare the photographs, and say why you think people choose to shop in places like these. All right?

Candidate B:	[*1 minute.*]
Interlocutor:	Thank you. *(Candidate A)*, do you enjoy shopping?
Candidate A:	[*Approximately 20 seconds.*]
Interlocutor:	Thank you.

Parts 3 and 4   7 minutes (9 minutes for groups of three)

Part 3

Life in the city

Interlocutor:	Now, I'd like you to talk about something together for about three minutes. *(4 minutes for groups of three.)*

Here are some pictures of things that can make living in a city enjoyable.

Indicate the set of pictures 2E on pages C6–C7 to the candidates.

First, talk to each other about how these things can help people to enjoy life in a city. Then decide which two things you think are the most important. All right?

Candidates:	[*3 minutes.*]
Interlocutor:	Thank you.

Part 4

Interlocutor: *Select any of the following questions as*
appropriate:

	Select any of the following
	prompts as appropriate:

* What are the disadvantages of living in a
  big city?
* Why do you think some people choose to
  live in the centre of cities?

* What do you think?
* Do you agree?
* And you?

* What is special about your capital city?
* Some people say that living in a city can be very lonely. What do you
  think?
* Would you prefer to live in a very modern city or an old one with lots of
  history? Why?
* Is there a city you would like to visit in the future? Why?

Thank you. That is the end of the test.

TEST 3

Note: In the examination, there will be both an assessor and an interlocutor in the room
   The visual material for **Test 3** appears on pages C9 and C12 (Part 2), and C10–C11 (Part 3).

Part 1   3 minutes (5 minutes for groups of three)

Interlocutor: Good morning/afternoon/evening. My name is .... and this is my
                  colleague ....
                  And your names are?
                  Can I have your mark sheets, please?
                  Thank you.
                  First of all, we'd like to know something about you.

* Where are you from *(Candidate A)*?
* And you *(Candidate B)*?
* What do you like about living *(here / name of candidate's home town)*?
* And what about you *(Candidate A/B)*?

Select one or more questions from any of the following categories, as appropriate.

Free time

* Are you an active person in your free time? (What sort of things do you do?)
* When did you last play a sport? (What was it?)

Travel

* Which country would you most like to visit? (Why?)
* Do you prefer going on holiday in a small group or a large group? (Why?)

Personal experience

* What is your favourite time of year? (Why?)
* Do you think you will always have the same friends? (Why? / Why not?)

Part 2   4 minutes (6 minutes for groups of three)

By the river
Preparing a meal

Interlocutor: In this part of the test, I'm going to give each of you two photographs.
                  I'd like you to talk about your photographs on your own for about a
                  minute, and also to answer a short question about your partner's
                  photographs.

                  (Candidate A), it's your turn first. Here are your photographs. They show
                  people spending time by different rivers.

Indicate pictures 3A and 3B on page C9 to Candidate A.

I'd like you to compare the photographs, and say what you think people are enjoying about spending time by these rivers. All right?

Candidate A:	[*1 minute.*]
Interlocutor:	Thank you. *(Candidate B)*, which of these rivers would you prefer to visit?
Candidate B:	[*Approximately 20 seconds.*]
Interlocutor:	Thank you.

Now, *(Candidate B)*, here are your two photographs. They show people preparing a meal in different situations.

Indicate pictures 3C and 3D on page C12 to Candidate B.

I'd like you to compare the photographs, and say what you think is difficult about preparing meals in these situations. All right?

Candidate B:	[*1 minute.*]
Interlocutor:	Thank you. *(Candidate A)*, do you enjoy cooking?
Candidate A:	[*Approximately 20 seconds.*]
Interlocutor:	Thank you.

Parts 3 and 4   7 minutes (9 minutes for groups of three)

Part 3

Community event

Interlocutor:	Now, I'd like you to talk about something together for about three minutes. (*4 minutes for groups of three.*)

I'd like you to imagine that some new houses have been built. The people living there want to get to know each other so they're organising a special event. Here are some of the ideas they are considering.

Indicate the set of pictures 3E on pages C10–C11 to the candidates.

First, talk to each other about how these ideas would help people to get to know each other. Then decide which idea would be the most successful. All right?

Candidates:	[*3 minutes.*]
Interlocutor	Thank you.

Part 4

Interlocutor: *Select any of the following questions as appropriate:*

- Which events do you think would be most difficult to organise? Why?
- What's the best way to get to know people? Why?

Select any of the following prompts as appropriate:

- What do you think?
- Do you agree?
- And you?

- Do people in your country organise activities like these? Why? / Why not?
- Do you think it's better to live in an old house or a new house? Why?
- How would you improve the area where you live?
- Do you think it's easier to make friends when you're a child? Why? / Why not?

Thank you. That is the end of the test.

Test 4

Note: In the examination, there will be both an assessor and an interlocutor in the room.
The visual material for **Test 4** appears on pages C15 and C16 (Part 2) and C14–C15 (Part 3).

Part 1   3 minutes (5 minutes for groups of three)

Interlocutor: Good morning/afternoon/evening. My name is .... and this is my
colleague................... .
And your names are?
Can I have your mark sheets, please?
Thank you.
First of all, we'd like to know something about you.

- Where are you from *(Candidate A)*?
- And you *(Candidate B)*?
- What do you like about living *(here / name of candidate's home town)*?
- And what about you *(Candidate A/B)*?

Select one or more questions from any of the following categories, as appropriate.

Personal experience

- Do you enjoy buying presents for people? (Is it ever difficult to buy for someone?)
- What was the best present you received recently? (Who gave it to you?)

Daily life

- Is your weekday routine different from your weekend routine? (In what ways?)
- What do you look forward to at the end of the day?

Media

- How much TV do you watch? (What kind of programmes do you <u>not</u> enjoy?)
- Do you buy magazines or newspapers regularly? (Why? / Why not?)

Part 2   4 minutes (6 minutes for groups of three)

Beaches
Adventure activities

Interlocutor: In this part of the test, I'm going to give each of you two photographs.
I'd like you to talk about your photographs on your own for about a
minute, and also to answer a short question about your partner's
photographs.

(Candidate A), it's your turn first. Here are your photographs. They show
two different beaches.

> *Indicate pictures 4A and 4B on page C13 to Candidate A.*
>
> I'd like you to compare the photographs, and say why you think people choose to go to beaches like these. All right?

Candidate A:	[*1 minute.*]
Interlocutor:	Thank you. *(Candidate B)*, which beach would you prefer to go to?
Candidate B:	[*Approximately 20 seconds.*]
Interlocutor:	Thank you.

> Now, *(Candidate B)*, here are your two photographs. They show people doing adventurous things.
>
> *Indicate pictures 4C and 4D on page C16 to Candidate B.*
>
> I'd like you to compare the photographs, and say what you think can be difficult about doing these things. All right?

Candidate B:	[*1 minute.*]
Interlocutor:	Thank you. *(Candidate A)*, would you like to do either of these things?
Candidate A:	[*Approximately 20 seconds.*]
Interlocutor:	Thank you.

Parts 3 and 4   7 minutes (9 minutes for groups of three)

Part 3

Olympic games

> Interlocutor: Now, I'd like you to talk about something together for about three minutes. *(4 minutes for groups of three.)*
>
> I'd like you to imagine the Olympic Games will take place in this country. Here are some of the jobs which young people could do.
>
> *Indicate the set of pictures 4E on pages C14–C15 to the candidates.*
>
> First, talk to each other about the advantages and disadvantages of the different jobs. Then decide which job would be the most interesting to do for a short time. All right?

Candidates:	[*3 minutes.*]
Interlocutor:	Thank you.

Part 4

Interlocutor: *Select any of the following questions as appropriate:*

<table>
<tr><td></td><td>*Select any of the following prompts as appropriate:*</td></tr>
</table>

Select any of the following questions as appropriate:

- What's more important, earning money or enjoying a job? Why?
- Why do you think some people have to wear uniforms at work?
- What do you think would be most interesting about working abroad? Why?
- Do you think languages can help people in their jobs? Why?
- How important is it to learn about different jobs when you are at school? Why?
- Would you prefer to work for a big or a small company? Why?

Select any of the following prompts as appropriate:

- What do you think?
- Do you agree?
- And you?

Thank you. That is the end of the test.

Marks and results

Paper 1   Reading

Candidates record their answers on a separate answer sheet. Two marks are given for each correct answer in **Parts 1 and 2** and one mark is given for each correct answer in **Part 3**. The total score is then weighted to 40 marks for the whole Reading paper.

Paper 2   Writing

General Impression Mark Scheme

A General Impression Mark Scheme is used in conjunction with a Task-specific Mark Scheme, which focuses on criteria specific to each particular task. The General Impression Mark Scheme summarises the content, organisation and cohesion, range of structures and vocabulary, register and format, and target reader indicated in each task.

A summary of the General Impression Mark Scheme is given below. Trained examiners, who are co-ordinated prior to each examination session, work with a more detailed version, which is subject to updating. The FCE General Impression Mark Scheme is interpreted at Council of Europe, Common European Framework Level B2.

Band 5	For a **Band 5** to be awarded, the candidate's writing fully achieves the desired effect on the target reader. All the content points required in the task are included* and expanded appropriately. Ideas are organised effectively, with the use of a variety of linking devices and a wide range of structure and vocabulary. The language is well developed, and any errors that do occur are minimal and perhaps due to ambitious attempts at more complex language. Register and format are consistently appropriate to the purpose of the task and the audience.
Band 4	For a **Band 4** to be awarded, the candidate's writing achieves the desired effect on the target reader. All the content points required in the task are included.* Ideas are clearly organised, with the use of suitable linking devices and a good range of structure and vocabulary. Generally, the language is accurate, and any errors that do occur are mainly attempts at more complex language. Register and format which are, on the whole, appropriate to the purpose of the task and the audience.
Band 3	For a **Band 3** to be awarded, the candidate's writing, on the whole, achieves the desired effect on the target reader. All the content points required in the task are included.* Ideas are organised adequately, with the use of simple linking devices and an adequate range of structure and vocabulary. A number of errors may be present, but they do not impede communication. A reasonable, if not always successful, attempt is made at register and format which are appropriate to the purpose of the task and the audience.
Band 2	For a **Band 2** to be awarded, the candidate's writing does not clearly communicate the message to the target reader. Some content points required in the task are inadequately covered or omitted, and/or there is some irrelevant material. Ideas are inadequately organised, linking devices are rarely used, and the range of structure and vocabulary is limited. Errors distract the reader and may obscure communication at times. Attempts at appropriate register and format are unsuccessful or inconsistent.

| Band 1 | For a **Band 1** to be awarded, the candidate's writing has a very negative effect on the target reader. There is notable omission of content points and/or considerable irrelevance, possibly due to misinterpretation of the task. There is a lack of organisation or linking devices, and there is little evidence of language control. The range of structure and vocabulary is narrow and frequent errors obscure communication. There is little or no awareness of appropriate register and format. |
| Band 0 | For a **Band zero** to be awarded, either there is too little language for assessment or the candidate's writing is totally irrelevant or totally illegible. |

*Candidates who do not address all the content points will be penalised for dealing inadequately with the requirements of the task.

Candidates who fully satisfy the **Band 3** descriptor are likely to demonstrate an adequate performance at FCE level.

Paper 2 sample answers and examiner's comments

The following pieces of writing have been selected from students' answers. The samples relate to tasks in Tests 1–4. Explanatory notes have been added to show how the bands have been arrived at. The comments should be read in conjunction with the task-specific mark schemes included in the keys.

Sample A (Test 1, Question 2 – Letter of Application)

Address

-

-

Date 18-6-05

International Book Shop Managor

Dear Mrs Benson

Re: Application

I am writing to apply for international Book Shop Job.

I saw your advertisement in an English language newspaper

I have certificate in English. I am intersting in reading books especially English book.

Last summer I worked in Tower Hamlet Book Shop which abeted me to developed a skills of working in difficult situation and team work.

I believed, I am a hard worker, good listener and friendly.

I look forward to hearing from you.

Your sincerely

Comments

Content
Reasonable achievement of task but is under 100 words.

Organisation and cohesion
Limited linking.

Range
Limited structures and vocabulary.

Accuracy
Some distracting errors.

Appropriacy of register and format
Successful attempt at register.

Target reader
Would have an idea of the candidate's suitability for the job.

Band: 2

Sample B (Test 1, Question 3 – Review)

> I usually not watch TV programmes because I prefer reading a book and seeing a film to watching TV but I always make sure to watch one programme on TV which is 'Open Concert'. It is a kind of music programme that shows once a week. 'Open Concert' is consist of sevral guests and a MC. The guests sing a song and talk with the MC about thier music which is like a real concert.
>
> last week I also saw that programme and the guest was very famos singer who songs lots of his song which was brilliant. I would like to see him again.
>
> However, they changed their programme's timetable which is a little bit confused because I didn't know that so I missed one which was three weeks ago. therefore I was a bit disappointed. They should have noticed but they didn't. Although they had a mistake, I still like this programme.

Comments

Content
Reasonable achievement of the task.

Organisation and cohesion
Suitably organised.

Range
A range of structure attempted.

Accuracy
A number of non-impeding errors.

Appropriacy of register and format
Appropriate to the task.

Target reader
Would be informed.

Band: 3

Sample C (Test 2, Question 1 – Email)

Dear Sam,

Thanks a lot for your email.

I'm sure your Art Course is very interesting. And I would like to help you with your painting. I have no time during the week, but why not come to my house at the weekend? As you know we have a huge colourful garden where we have enough space. I'll wear the neckless which I inherited from my grandmother. I loved her very much and it is very precious to me.

I would ask you, if there is anything what you need, as a chair, for example? Also would you like to have dinner with us, because the paining will may take some time and we'll be hungry afterwards.

I look forward to your return emaill!

Love

Nicole

Comments

Content
All content points included.

Organisation and cohesion
Well organised.

Range
A very good range of structure and vocabulary.

Accuracy
Very accurate.

Appropriacy of register and format
Fully appropriate to the task.

Target reader
Would be fully informed.

Band: 5

Sample D (Test 3, Question 3 – Story)

> Tina was standing near the window waiting to be called by the president of 'The singer's dreams". She always had been keen on music and specially on singing. For that reason, she was interesting in the idea of taking part in a new musicians and singer's quiz.
>
> So there she was, exhausted because of the nerves. The others girls in the competition were more young and beautiful than she was. But she knew she had a nice voice. During the competition the ambient wasn't relax at all. Anybody was friendly but at least anybody was disturbing her.
>
> The silence in the room was broken by a man who said that the jury was near to make a choice. So she left the small room and she took place in front of the jury.
>
> A smart lady announce the name of the winners and Tina was one of them.
>
> <u>She was very excited when she heard</u> that <u>she had won the prize</u>. Her dream has became true.

Comments

Content
Storyline well developed. Final sentence is a comment to round off the story.

Organisation and cohesion
Story flows, with appropriate paragraphing.

Range
Sustained runs of language with appropriate vocabulary e.g. 'The silence ... was broken ... jury ...'.

Accuracy
Variable. A few basic errors.

Appropriacy of register and format
Appropriate.

Target reader
Would follow the storyline.

Band: 3

Sample E (Test 3, Question 4 – Article)

> I don't know if I have found the perfect holiday destination but I'm sure that Watamu is the best place I have ever visited.
>
> Watamu is a small village on the coastline of Kenya. It takes three hours to arrive there by car from the capital Nairobi but it's a trip that is worth to be done.
>
> When I booked the holiday I thought I was going to spend all the time laying on the beach. I was wrong! Once arrived there I discovered a lots of way to have fun. The sea and the white beaches with the palms are stunning but there something more you can enjoy. The countryside is also interesting and people are friendly and sell the products of their poor country always smiling.
>
> And you cannot imagine how amazing is to make a safari in the park. Because of the very hot temperature, you have to set out very early in the morning if you want to see all the animals. The landscape of the park is fascinating, everything seems to very dry, there are no trees just bushes. Driving on your jeep you discover something really special: a wild world full of life.

Comments

Content
Full realisation of the task, with appropriate expansion.

Organisation and cohesion
Effectively organised with a strong, positive ending.

Range
Wide range e.g. 'the white beaches ... are stunning'. Relevant vocabulary.

Accuracy
Minimal errors. Good control.

Appropriacy of register and format
Good article style.

Target reader
Would be fully informed.

Band: 5

Paper 3 Use of English

One mark is given for each correct answer in **Parts 1, 2** and **3**. For **Part 4**, candidates are awarded a mark of 2, 1 or 0 for each question according to the accuracy of their response. Correct spelling is required in **Parts 2, 3** and **4**. The total mark is subsequently weighted to 40.

Paper 4 Listening

One mark is given for each correct answer. The total is weighted to give a mark out of 40 for the paper. In **Part 2** minor spelling errors are allowed, provided that the candidate's intention is clear.

For security reasons, several versions of the Listening paper are used at each administration of the examination. Before grading, the performance of the candidates in each of the versions is compared and marks adjusted to compensate for any imbalance in levels of difficulty.

Paper 5 Speaking

Candidates are assessed on their own individual performance and not in relation to each other, according to the following four analytical critera: grammar and vocabulary, discourse management, pronunciation and interactive communication. Assessment is based on performance in the whole test and not in particular parts of the test.

Both examiners assess the candidates. The assessor applies detailed, analytical scales, and the interlocutor applies a global achievement scale, which is based on the analytical scales.

Analytical scores

Grammar and Vocabulary

This refers to the accurate and appropriate use of a range of grammatical forms and vocabulary. Performance is viewed in terms of the overall effectiveness of the language used in spoken interaction.

Discourse Management

This refers to the candidate's ability to link utterances together to form coherent speech, without undue hesitation. The utterances should be relevant to the tasks and should be arranged logically to develop the themes or arguments required by the tasks.

Pronunciation

This refers to the candidate's ability to produce intelligible utterances to fulfil the task requirements. This includes stress and intonation as well as individual sounds. Examiners put themselves in the position of the non-ESOL specialist and assess the overall impact of the pronunciation and the degree of effort required to understand the candidate.

Interactive Communication

This refers to the candidate's ability to take an active part in the development of the discourse. This requires the ability to participate in the range of interactive situations in the test and to develop discussions on a range of topics by initiating and responding appropriately. This also refers to the deployment of strategies to maintain interaction at an appropriate level throughout the test so that the tasks can be fulfilled.

Global Achievement

This refers to the candidate's overall effectiveness in dealing with the tasks in the four separate parts of the FCE Speaking test. The global mark is an independent, impression mark which reflects the assessment of the candidate's performance from the interlocutor's perspective.

Marks

Marks for each of the criteria are awarded out of a nine-point scale. Marks for the Speaking test are subsequently weighted to produce a final mark out of 40.

FCE typical minimum adequate performance

Although there are some inaccuracies, grammar and vocabulary are sufficiently accurate in dealing with the tasks. The language is mostly coherent, with some extended discourse. Candidates can generally be understood. They are able to maintain the interaction and deal with the tasks without major prompting.

Test 1 Key

Paper 1   Reading (1 hour)

Part 1

1 D   2 A   3 B   4 A   5 C   6 B   7 D   8 B

Part 2

9 C   10 H   11 A   12 E   13 B   14 G   15 F

Part 3

16 D   17 C   18 A   19 C   20 A   21 B   22 A   23 B   24 D
25 A   26 C   27 B   28 D   29 C   30 D

Paper 2   Writing (1 hour 20 minutes)

Task-specific Mark Schemes

Part 1

Question 1

Content
The letter should include all the points in the notes:
1) make positive comment about sports camp
2) state preference for sleeping arrangements
3) give details of something to cook
4) tell Robin what writer would like to do before the camp.

Organisation and cohesion
Clear organisation of ideas, with suitable paragraphing, linking and
opening/closing formulae as appropriate to the task.

Range
Language relating to the functions above.
Vocabulary relating to making arrangements and sports camp.

Appropriacy of register and format
Standard English appropriate to the situation and target reader observing grammar
and spelling conventions.

Target reader
Would be informed.

Part 2

Question 2

Content
The letter should relate to the job in the bookshop.

Organisation and cohesion
Clear organisation of ideas, with suitable paragraphing and linking with suitable opening and closing formulae.

Range
Language of explanation, description and giving information.
Vocabulary relating to books, reading and work experience.

Appropriacy of register and format
Consistent register suitable to the situation and target reader.

Target reader
Would be informed.

Question 3

Content
The review should give details of writer's favourite TV programme.

Organisation and cohesion
Clear organisation of ideas, with suitable paragraphing and linking.

Range
Language of describing, explaining and giving opinion.

Appropriacy of register and format
Consistent register suitable to the situation and target reader.

Target reader
Would be informed.

Question 4

Content
The story should continue from the prompt sentence.

Organisation and cohesion
Storyline should be clear. Paragraphing could be minimal.

Range
Narrative tenses. Vocabulary appropriate to the chosen topic of story.

Appropriacy of register and format
Consistent register suitable to the story.

Target reader
Would be able to follow the storyline.

Question 5(a)

Content
The essay should describe a situation where Andrew Manson faces difficulty and how he deals with this.

Organisation and cohesion
Clear organisation of ideas, with suitable paragraphing and linking.

Range
Language of description and explanation.
Vocabulary relating to the situation chosen from the book.

Appropriacy of register and format
Consistent register suitable to the situation and target reader.

Target reader
Would be informed.

Question 5(b)

Content
The letter should respond to the suggestion that travel was more enjoyable in the period of *Around the World in 80 Days*.

Organisation and cohesion
Clear organisation of ideas, with suitable paragraphing and linking.

Range
Language of opinion and description.
Vocabulary relating to travel and the events in the book.

Appropriacy of register and format
Consistent register suitable to the situation and target reader.

Target reader
Would be informed.

Paper 3   Use of English (45 minutes)

Part 1

1 C   2 D   3 A   4 D   5 A   6 C   7 D   8 C   9 A   10 C   11 A   12 B

Part 2

13 would / could / might   14 what   15 any / every   16 as   17 up / down   18 of
19 all / everything   20 taking   21 for / in   22 because   23 if   24 than

Part 3

25 knowledge   26 toughest   27 scientific   28 suffering   29 comfortably
30 unlike   31 relatively   32 energetic   33 additional   34 warmth

Part 4

35 in **order** | not to   36 are/'re **required** | to show your   37 **soon** as | I get
38 **more** than five/5 years | since   39 **rather** drive home | than stay   40 keep/get/have
his skis | **under** control   41 **said** to | have been   42 a **few** players/people | have
achieved

Paper 4   Listening (approximately 40 minutes)

Part 1

1 B   2 C   3 C   4 B   5 A   6 B   7 C   8 A

Part 2

9 travel agent('s) / travel agency   10 poster   11 Changes   12 (local) (African)
farmers   13 three / 3 weeks   14 motorbike / motorcycle   15 (the) (local) women
16 traffic (noise)   17 (pieces of) furniture   18 gardening

Part 3

19 E   20 A   21 D   22 B   23 F

Part 4

24 C   25 C   26 B   27 A   28 A   29 C   30 B

Transcript   *This is the Cambridge First Certificate in English Listening Test. Test One.*

I'm going to give you the instructions for this test.
I'll introduce each part of the test and give you time to look at the questions.
At the start of each piece you'll hear this sound:

tone

You'll hear each piece twice.

Remember, while you're listening, write your answers on the question paper.
You'll have five minutes at the end of the test to copy your answers onto the
separate answer sheet.

There will now be a pause. Please ask any questions now, because you must
not speak during the test.

[pause]

Now open your question paper and look at Part One.

[pause]

PART 1   *You'll hear people talking in eight different situations. For questions 1 to 8,*
choose the best answer, A, B or C.

Question 1   One.
You hear a restaurant manager talking about the cooks who work for him.
What does he say about them?
A They dislike cleaning tasks.
B They have a choice of jobs.
C They help to decide the menu.

[pause]

tone

As restaurant manager, I feel responsible for the quality of the food we serve. So it's up to me to check the ingredients that have been delivered overnight to make sure they are of sufficient quality, and to produce a menu for the day. The cooks arrive at about ten a.m. to prepare lunch and I'll take them through the menu. Because lunch is concentrated over a short period of time it can get very busy and very hot. But unlike some kitchens, we tend to divide the jobs up according to who likes doing what, and that includes cleaning pots and pans and clearing the place before dinner.

[pause]

tone

[The recording is repeated.]

[pause]

Question 2   Two.
You hear a woman talking about a new book.
What does she particularly like about the book?
A It is educational.
B It is well organised.
C It is enjoyable.

[pause]

tone

It's a factual book, a chronicle of the twentieth century and it's wonderful. I mean it's terribly bitty and it's not going to give you a lot of information nor be good for school work. That's what's really nice about it. Here is a reference book which it is fun to dip in and out of. It's hardly going to help anyone write an essay and it avoids being geared to any school syllabus, unlike so much of what is published today. But for anyone who likes little details, you know, you can look up your date of birth, for example, and see what else happened then, it's a very good book.

[pause]

tone

[The recording is repeated.]

[pause]

Question 3 *Three.*
You hear the writer of a television soap opera being interviewed about the programme.
What will happen next in the story?
A Someone will make an important decision.
B Someone will go away unexpectedly.
C Someone will learn the truth at last.

[pause]

tone

Man: So, there've been some dramatic events in Victoria Street this past week, what with Mariela deciding not to marry Jason, and Stephen leaving home in the middle of a family row. Are next week's episodes as exciting?
Woman: Well, I can't give away the whole story, but I don't think you'll be disappointed! I can tell you that Stephen's mother is forced to tell her husband the secret she's been hiding for years, which leads to more fireworks and a few tears. And Jason refuses to accept Mariela's decision, so you're going to hear a lot more from him, and look out for some surprises there.

[pause]

tone

[The recording is repeated.]

[pause]

Question 4 *Four.*
You hear part of a radio interview.
Who is speaking?
A a taxi driver
B a porter
C a tourist guide

[pause]

tone

We get people to the taxis, that's the first priority, and to the trains. We make sure they get on early and get comfortable seats. These days many passengers have a lot of luggage and they want assistance with it. So we provide a much-needed service. We even take people down to the Underground or to places in the surrounding streets. But the majority of users are airline passengers with a lot of bags and perhaps accompanied by elderly relatives, young children and so on. Obviously they can't manage everything on their own.

[pause]

tone

[The recording is repeated.]

[pause]

Question 5

Five.
You hear a woman talking about how she keeps fit.
Why did she decide to take up line dancing?
A She thought the pace would suit her.
B She had heard about it on television.
C She wanted to try exercising to music.

[pause]

tone

I exercise in the form of dance. At one time, I did aerobics because exercise is more interesting with music, but I've since moved on to line dancing. It's less energetic, but I go three times a week. I run my own business, work hard, and it's just a way to cut off rather than watch television. It's also a challenge keeping up with the new steps. I think young people sometimes take exercise too far, get over-concerned with how they look, when they'll never be able to keep it up at that sort of pace. Whereas line dancing struck me as something I could sustain as part of my normal life.

[pause]

tone

[The recording is repeated.]

[pause]

Question 6

Six.
You overhear a conversation in a restaurant.
What does the woman think about the food she has just eaten?
A It was expensive.
B It was delicious.
C It looked wonderful.

[pause]

tone

Man: Well, what did you think of that, then?
Woman: Brilliant! I've never tasted anything like it! I wish now I'd tried this place sooner. I mean, I've been walking past it for years.
Man: Why didn't you?
Woman: Well, to be honest, I never thought I'd be able to afford it, but it's actually quite reasonable. Mind you, I think they could have tried a bit harder with the presentation. I think if food looks good on the plate you automatically expect it to taste good. Yours was okay, but I think they could have made more of an effort with mine.

[pause]

tone

[The recording is repeated.]

[pause]

Question 7   *Seven.*
You turn on the radio and hear a man talking.
What is he talking about?
A drawing pictures
B writing fiction
C composing music

[pause]

tone

In practical terms, the place I'm in doesn't matter too much. As long as I have the necessary tools, you know, pencil and paper and, of course, my keyboard. Once I'm started, I go over things again and again – must be very dull if anyone's listening. I change a few notes here and there, but basically I tend to stick with an idea once I have it. I guess home's the best place in a way because there I'm relaxed enough to let my imagination flow and that's what you need to do, in order to produce a good piece …

[pause]

tone

[The recording is repeated.]

[pause]

Question 8   *Eight.*
You overhear a student phoning her parents.
What is her opinion of the place she is living in while at college?
A She is not sure she will have enough room to study.
B She has difficulty in working because of the noise.
C She does not get on well with her room-mates.

[pause]

tone

Well, I'm sharing with two other girls … I know, it was supposed to be me and one other person, but there's a shortage of accommodation, apparently. Anyway, the room's rather cramped. But it's great. There've been three parties so far, and it's still the first week. It's an incredibly noisy place, with doors banging and people laughing and shouting till the small hours. Yes, I suppose we'll have to get down to work soon, though I don't know how we'll be able to, packed into that little space – none of us is very tidy …

[pause]

tone

[The recording is repeated.]

[pause]

That's the end of Part One.

Now turn to Part Two.

[pause]

PART 2   *You'll hear an interview with Elizabeth Holmes about her experience working in Africa. For questions 9 to 18, complete the sentences.*

You now have forty-five seconds in which to look at Part Two.

[pause]

tone

Interviewer: Visitors to the small Devon village of Whimple might be forgiven for looking twice as they pass the garden of Elizabeth Holmes. In the middle of the garden there stands a traditional African hut, a reminder of the two years Elizabeth spent in Africa as a volunteer. Elizabeth, what persuaded you to leave your secure job in a travel agent's and go to Africa?

Elizabeth: Well, I'd been feeling restless for ages. I wanted to see the real world, not just tourist places. Then, I was at the dentist's one day, waiting to go in, and I'd read all the magazines in the waiting room, so I started looking at a poster – it was all about volunteers working in Africa.

Interviewer: And it interested you?

Elizabeth: Yes, I took down the name and address and applied. I had an interview locally and did some aptitude tests. Then just before I left for Africa, there was a training weekend in London, which they call 'Changes' and which gives you some idea of what you're letting yourself in for.

Interviewer: What particular skills could you offer?

Elizabeth: I had a degree in economics and I had done some teaching at one time. What they wanted to send me to Africa to do was to train local farmers in the marketing of their produce. I flew out with fifteen other volunteers, all going to do different things, like nursing, teaching, and so on. When we got there, we were supposed to have a four-week course at a training centre learning something about the local culture and the basics of the language – you know, greetings and things like that. Anyway, there was a problem and it only lasted three weeks in the end – not enough really.

Interviewer: Did it take a long time to get used to your new lifestyle?

Elizabeth: I found it quite difficult for the first few weeks, but after that I settled in very well. My area covered 1200 square kilometres, and I had a truck for long-distance travel, but for more local trips I rode a motorbike.

Interviewer: How did you get on with the local people?

Elizabeth: Very well. The men were very polite but they tended to keep their distance – unlike the women, who were always inviting me to meals. They showed me how they wove and dyed material to make clothes for themselves and their children. I used to get magazines sent from England and we'd spend ages looking at them.

Interviewer: I expect you found it very different when you returned to England?

Elizabeth: Yes, I certainly did. After two years of living very simply, I found the supermarkets especially overwhelming – just the enormous choice of food. Also, the traffic disturbed me. I had to move from my flat in the city to a small cottage in the country just to get some of the peace and quiet I'd become accustomed to in Africa.

Interviewer: And what are you working on at the moment?

Elizabeth: Well, I didn't want to just go back to working in someone else's office so I set up my own business, which I run from home. I deal in African furniture. I brought some small pieces back with me as souvenirs and everyone loved them in Britain. However, I'm still in touch with the organisation that sent me to Africa as a volunteer. I organise events to raise funds and give talks about my experience to encourage other people to go.

Interviewer: Has the experience in Africa changed you at all?

Elizabeth: Oh yes, in many ways. I used to spend all my time working, but now I make sure I have more time for gardening – my favourite hobby.

Interviewer: Well, I'd like to thank Elizabeth for coming into the studio today. If you're interested in ...

[pause]

Now you'll hear Part Two again.

tone

[The recording is repeated.]

[pause]

That's the end of Part Two.

Now turn to Part Three.

[pause]

PART 3   *You'll hear five different employees talking about what makes a good boss. For questions 19 to 23, choose which of the opinions, A to F, each speaker expresses. Use the letters only once. There is one extra letter which you do not need to use.*

You now have thirty seconds in which to look at Part Three.

[pause]

tone

Speaker 1

Man: Some people still think that leaders are born, not made. They say, no matter how hard you study and how many diplomas you collect, at the end of the day, if you've got natural skills, such as a strong character, that's all you'll need. I think that's nonsense. Leadership is all about commanding respect. If a boss says to me, for example, 'Look, your computer skills need upgrading',

I'll think, 'Right, this person has a degree in computing, I don't, so he must be right'. But if it's the other way round, then you feel, well, maybe I should be boss!

[pause]

Speaker 2

Woman: Well, the sort of leaders that I actually admire ... are not the ... top dogs in suits ... with a degree in management and a belief that nobody can do things as well as they can. One thing I've learned from all my experience in different jobs is that, to be a really good boss, you have to be good at encouraging the people under you to decide on important issues ... creating a situation in which other people can shine. Of course this does not mean the boss's job is any easier; it's still a challenge, but so much more rewarding for everyone.

[pause]

Speaker 3

Woman: Since I left school, I've done a number of short-term office jobs, and I must say I'm beginning to realise how important it is to have the right sort of person directing your work. To develop all my potential, I need to be told when I'm doing something well, and also the areas where I could improve ... I think the earlier you get formal and informal feedback, the better. Otherwise you develop bad habits ... some of my workmates don't agree with me, when I say it's good to meet regularly with your boss, they think I'm trying to be better than them.

[pause]

Speaker 4

Man: Of course we all want bosses who are knowledgeable and who bring energy to the job, and I must say, in my opinion, most people who reach top job positions do possess these qualities. However, what really matters is the ability to bring people together. Leaders often mistakenly encourage people to work on their own, kind of, in isolation, because they are afraid of the strengths of groups, they think maybe they'll criticise, or even join forces against the leader ... Such leaders need to go on management courses, to look at good examples of leadership ...

[pause]

Speaker 5

Man: Well, in the organisation where I work, each department has a leader, a boss ... and because I've worked in six of these departments, I've had six different bosses! I must say there's been very little to complain about ... except that we are being asked to do an enormous amount of extra work and some of the bosses don't seem to be doing long hours, like the rest of us. It is true that after work, they may have to attend special management courses, or meet individual members of staff to discuss performance, but this only happens occasionally …

[pause]

Now you'll hear Part Three again.

tone

[The recording is repeated.]

[pause]

That's the end of Part Three.

Now turn to Part Four.

[pause]

PART 4

You'll hear an interview with Trina Trevose, a pop singer, who is only 15. For questions 24 to 30, choose the best answer, A, B or C.

You now have one minute in which to look at Part Four.

[pause]

tone

Interviewer:	... Trina, you're 15 and you've just come back from America where you've been making records. What was it like?
Trina:	It was wonderful. I had the six-week school summer holidays and, you know, went over there for a month and then started school again.
Interviewer:	What did your classmates at school think?
Trina:	I just told close friends what I was doing in the States ... And I thought, well, if the records were successful, *then* I'd tell everyone ...
Interviewer:	And they were successful.
Trina:	Right. And my friends were very good about it. Not envious, or anything.
Interviewer:	Did you like being in the USA?
Trina:	Oh, yes, most of the time it was great – the people are so friendly.
Interviewer:	Did you manage to write any songs there?
Trina:	Well, yeah, I did. Most of the stuff I'd done in England had been about the people closest to me – you know, Mum, Dad, my sister. They weren't with me in the States, and although I missed them and silly things like the rain in England and fish and chips, being surrounded with new faces gave me lots of material for my songs.
Interviewer:	Now, your home in England is a long way from London.
Trina:	Yes, about as far as you can get!
Interviewer:	So, is it easy to get into the music business if you live that far away? Don't you have to be in London or near a big city at least?
Trina:	No, no. We did play in London once but we were actually approached at a local concert, so I don't think it's impossible to get noticed anywhere. There are lots of record companies looking for bands, and they do go quite a long way from the cities to find them. I was lucky with my band, and there have

been other bands like us that've been lucky as well, so you don't have to come from a huge city to be discovered.

Interviewer:	Now, in the USA you did a song with someone who was a star when I was your age, David Pearson, and you hadn't any idea who he was?
Trina:	No. It was embarrassing, actually. But he was a really pleasant guy. He was recording an album in the same studio, and he had this song that he needed someone to sing with him, and he asked me, and I was only too delighted to do it!
Interviewer:	But that wasn't the only famous star you worked with in the States, was it?
Trina:	No, there was Lance Lakatoff.
Interviewer:	But you *had* heard of him ...
Trina:	Yes. He's a bit of a hero of mine, in fact.
Interviewer:	And you were in his TV series?
Trina:	Yes.
Interviewer:	And what was that like?
Trina:	It was a really good experience. I hadn't done anything like that before. And they filmed us for three or four days, you know. That was the end of it. Or so I thought! But they had made some mistakes, which was such a shame. Because I had to go back to the USA! I came home to England, and then they phoned up and said they had some bad camera work, etc., and I had to fly all the way back and do it again ...
Interviewer:	Actually, in the USA your record did well. But not here in England. Why's that?
Trina:	Because you've never been able to get it over here in Britain. The record company's never had any arrangements to sell their records in Britain, so it's always just been the USA, which is nice in a way.
Interviewer:	Why do you say that?
Trina:	Well, it's good to come home and get away from it.
Interviewer:	But is it that the company don't think your style will appeal over here?
Trina:	No, it's purely the fact they don't operate over here. But the company's just been sold, and the new company does operate over here, so maybe they will release the record.
Interviewer:	So, where do you see your career going? Will you go back to the States?
Trina:	Well, not for a while I shouldn't think, as I have another two years at school here in England. I know my schoolfriends are thinking of college but I'm not sure that's for me, even to do music. Then, my agent has been trying to persuade me to do it full time, and my parents say it's up to me, but I'm happy to wait a while before that happens. I can still write, after all – in fact, one of my songs is in the American charts at the moment, but sung by someone else.
Interviewer:	Well, the best of luck, Trina, and now ...

[pause]

Now you'll hear Part Four again.

tone

[The recording is repeated.]

[pause]

That's the end of Part Four.

There'll now be a pause of five minutes for you to copy your answers onto the separate answer sheet. Be sure to follow the numbering of all the questions. I'll remind you when there is one minute left, so that you are sure to finish in time.

[Teacher, pause the recording here for five minutes. Remind your students when they have one minute left.]

That's the end of the test. Please stop now. Your supervisor will now collect all the question papers and answer sheets.

Test 2 Key

Paper 1   Reading (1 hour)

Part 1

1 B   2 A   3 D   4 C   5 A   6 C   7 B   8 B

Part 2

9 D   10 H   11 E   12 C   13 F   14 B   15 G

Part 3

16 C   17 B   18 B   19 A   20 C   21 A   22 D   23 D   24 C
25 C   26 A   27 D   28 B   29 A   30 D

Paper 2   Writing (1 hour 20 minutes)

Task-specific Mark Schemes

Part 1

Question 1

Content
The email should include all the points in the notes:
1) express enthusiasm for the idea of being painted
2) describe a suitable place for the painting
3) give details of object
4) ask an additional question.

Organisation and cohesion
Clear organisation of ideas, with suitable paragraphing, linking and opening/closing formulae as appropriate to the task.

Range
Language relating to the functions above.
Vocabulary relating to making arrangements and art course.

Appropriacy of register and format
Standard English appropriate to the situation and target reader, observing grammar and spelling conventions.

Target reader
Would be informed.

Part 2

Question 2

Content
The report should give information about camping in local area.

Organisation and cohesion
Clear organisation of ideas, with suitable paragraphing and linking. Headings an advantage but not essential.

Range
Language of explanation and description.
Vocabulary relating to camping.

Appropriacy of register and format
Consistent register suitable to the situation and target reader.

Target reader
Would be informed.

Question 3

Content
The letter should give information about writer's use of internet.

Organisation and cohesion
Clear organisation of ideas, with suitable paragraphing and linking.

Range
Language of describing, explaining and expressing opinion.

Appropriacy of register and format
Consistent register suitable to the situation and target reader.

Target reader
Would be informed.

Question 4

Content
The review should give details of writer's CD.

Organisation and cohesion
Clear organisation of ideas, with suitable paragraphing and linking.

Range
Language of describing, explaining and giving opinion.

Appropriacy of register and format
Consistent register suitable to the situation and target reader.

Target reader
Would be informed.

Question 5(a)

Content
The article should give details of the relationship.

Organisation and cohesion
Clear organisation of ideas, with suitable paragraphing and linking.

Range
Language of description and opinion.
Vocabulary relating to Andrew and Christine.

Appropriacy of register and format
Consistent register suitable to the situation and target reader.

Target reader
Would be informed.

Question 5(b)

Content
The essay should describe the most exciting adventure from the book.

Organisation and cohesion
Clear organisation of ideas, with suitable paragraphing and linking.

Range
Language of description and opinion.
Vocabulary relating to the chosen adventure in the book.

Appropriacy of register and format
Consistent register suitable to the situation and target reader.

Target reader
Would be informed.

Paper 3   Use of English (45 minutes)

Part 1

1 A   2 C   3 D   4 B   5 B   6 A   7 D   8 C   9 C   10 C
11 A   12 B

Part 2

13 When   14 had   15 great / good   16 as / for   17 each   18 At
19 make   20 not   21 to   22 well   23 way   24 whether / if

Part 3

25 delightful   26 choice   27 impressive   28 highly   29 attractions
30 annually   31 stormy   32 unsuitable   33 easily   34 reliable

Part 4

35 is no/not / isn't any **difference** | between   **36** it was/would be | **necessary** for
37 how | **high** the mountain   **38** any (more) | paper **left**   **39** not **having /**
having not | done   **40** be/go | on **sale**   **41** **even** though | it/the weather was
42 looked **up** | to

Paper 4   Listening (approximately 40 minutes)

Part 1

1 C   **2** B   **3** B   **4** A   **5** A   **6** C   **7** A   **8** C

Part 2

9 National Museum   **10** final / last   **11** glass work / glass   **12** industrial
13 gun   **14** waiter   **15** film(s) / movies   **16** computer company   **17** metal
18 (old) maps

Part 3

19 B   **20** A   **21** F   **22** D   **23** E

Part 4

24 B   **25** A   **26** C   **27** A   **28** B   **29** C   **30** C

Transcript   *This is the Cambridge First Certificate in English Listening Test. Test Two.*

I'm going to give you the instructions for this test.
I'll introduce each part of the test and give you time to look at the questions.
At the start of each piece you'll hear this sound:

tone

You'll hear each piece twice.

Remember, while you're listening, write your answers on the question paper.
You'll have five minutes at the end of the test to copy your answers onto the
separate answer sheet.

There will now be a pause. Please ask any questions now, because you must
not speak during the test.

[pause]

Now open your question paper and look at Part One.

[pause]

PART 1   *You'll hear people talking in eight different situations. For questions 1 to 8,*
                choose the best answer, A, B or C.

Question 1   One.
                You overhear a woman talking to her husband on a mobile phone.
                What is the background to the conversation?
                A The family's holiday may have to be cancelled.
                B The woman wants to buy their son a computer.
                C Their son has schoolwork to complete before the start of term.

                [pause]

                tone

                Listen, about Jimmy's school project. I spoke to the computer department at
                work about borrowing a laptop, and apparently they're only supposed to give
                them out to people on company business. So I guess Jimmy will just have to
                write it all out by hand and type it out when we get back. That'll only give him
                two days, but what can we do? I know he's been at home all summer, but
                that's Jimmy for you, and he's only twelve. I just wish his school was a bit
                more understanding about people's holiday arrangements.

                [pause]

                tone

                [The recording is repeated.]

                [pause]

Question 2   Two.
                You hear a phone-in programme on the radio.
                Why has the man phoned?
                A to complain about the traffic scheme
                B to express his support for the traffic scheme
                C to question the aims of the traffic scheme

                [pause]

                tone

Woman: Go ahead, Paul, I'm listening.
   Man: Well ... I'm fed up with listening to all your callers moaning on about the new
          traffic scheme. I mean, that woman who said it took fifty minutes to cross the
          city by car instead of her usual thirty. Poor thing! Why doesn't she leave
          the car at home and use the bus service instead? Anyway, the aim of the
          new scheme isn't to make car journeys quicker; it's for shoppers and
          pedestrians and cyclists and bus passengers, and it's working. I recommend
          everyone to have a walk in the city centre and see for themselves. That's all
          I wanted to say.

          [pause]

tone

[The recording is repeated.]

[pause]

Question 3

Three.
On the radio, you hear a woman talking about her house.
What has she recently done?
A decided to move to another area
B solved a problem that she had
C made improvements to her house

[pause]

tone

I do sometimes think about moving, I can't deny it, but when you've lived in a house for as long as I have, you learn to accept its drawbacks and you stop always trying to change things. Here, the garden is a bit big for me to cope with as I would like, but now I've got someone who comes in once a week to help me out, and things have definitely improved, so I think I'll be staying put for just a little bit longer.

[pause]

tone

[The recording is repeated.]

[pause]

Question 4

Four.
You overhear two people discussing a friend.
What language does their friend usually speak at home?
A French
B English
C Italian

[pause]

tone

Man: I had dinner at Mark's house last night. His father made a delicious Italian dessert.

Woman: Oh, yes, his parents are Italian, aren't they? I keep forgetting that because Mark's English is so good.

Man: Of course it is! He was born in Texas. And his mother's not Italian, she's French. That's what they all speak to each other, though they used English when I was there. Mark has to go to classes on Saturdays to learn to read and write Italian. To hear him speak on the phone to his grandmother in Rome, you'd think it was his first language!

[pause]

tone

[The recording is repeated.]

[pause]

Question 5   *Five.*
You hear a man talking about an activity holiday he went on as a child
with his family.
How did he feel during the holiday?
A bored by the climbing
B upset with his father
C disappointed with the rowing boat

[pause]

tone

As a child all our holidays were in Scotland because my father was very keen on climbing and he insisted we went climbing every day. One day the weather stopped us going climbing, much to my relief, so we hired a rowing boat on the lake. My father complained it was uncomfortable and slow (he preferred motorboats) but I sat there and thought, 'This feels good!' – even though the boat was old and creaky. After that, I just got the bug really ... and I've been rowing ever since. And the boats now are better than that first one in Scotland!

[pause]

tone

[The recording is repeated.]

[pause]

Question 6   *Six.*
You hear the beginning of a radio programme.
What is the programme going to be about?
A child development
B the environment
C a form of entertainment

[pause]

tone

As any parent or childcarer knows, it's pointless buying drums or expensive instruments for small children; give them a wooden spoon, a saucepan lid and a cardboard box, and they'll happily bang away for hours. So you could say that the group named Thump are simply having their second childhood. Just over seven years ago, this small band of street performers from the north of England decided to turn their routine with metal rubbish bins and bicycle chains into a stage show. They now have five separate groups working nightly across the country and are just about to begin their first tour of the USA.

[pause]

tone

[The recording is repeated.]

[pause]

Question 7

Seven.
You hear a man being interviewed about a new project he has set up.
What is the purpose of the project?
A to help people find accommodation in Scotland
B to tell people where to stay in Australia
C to advise people how to set up a flat agency

[pause]

tone

Woman: Mark, this new project you've got, this flat agency, has this arisen from your own experience, or what?

Man: Both from bitter personal experience of having to find somewhere to live in Edinburgh over the last few years – crossing the city from one corner to the next and turning up at hundreds of places which weren't suitable ... and also it was taken from an idea in Australia where a similar service was set up and I thought, 'Well, let's try and take out some of the misery of trying to find a flat here in Scotland.'

[pause]

tone

[The recording is repeated.]

[pause]

Question 8

Eight.
You switch on the radio in the middle of a programme.
What kind of programme is it?
A an arts review
B an interview
C a quiz show

[pause]

tone

Woman: And now, Mr Harman, what I want to ask you is in which of Shakespeare's plays does the character Queen Titania appear?

Man: Mmm, now let me think for a moment. Well, it was one of the comedies. I believe she was a fairy ...

Woman:	I can tell you that it was performed at the Regent Theatre last year starring Eveline Thomas and had excellent reviews.
Man:	I don't remember that. Now, is it *Midsummer Night's Dream*, by William Shakespeare?
Woman:	Indeed it is.

[pause]

tone

[The recording is repeated.]

[pause]

That's the end of Part One.

Now turn to Part Two.

[pause]

PART 2   *You'll hear an announcement about an evening's programmes on Radio Pearl. For questions 9 to 18, complete the sentences.*

You now have forty-five seconds in which to look at Part Two.

[pause]

tone

And now a look at some of this evening's programmes on Radio Pearl. At 7.30 we have *Art Review*, a programme which has fast become a favourite among our listeners, with its mix of in-depth reports on artistic events, and revealing interviews with the artists who regularly come into the studio. Today we'll be going to London to the National Museum, which holds approximately five events a year, and this particular one is always popular because it features work by student artists.

This year is no exception as everything is the work of final-year art students from a local college. You'll be surprised at the variety of things you can see. Exhibits range from curtains to glass work, and I understand there are a total of nearly 2,000 works on display. There is an excellent use of raw materials and of course many exhibits demonstrate how industrial technology can be employed in art. If you want to buy any of the exhibits, it will cost you anything from £25 up to £2,000. So for more information on what can be seen, where and for how much, tune in to Radio Pearl tonight at 7.30.

Then at 8.00, there's another in our series of classic plays and tonight it's *The Vanishing Lady*, starring Margaret Louden.

Briefly, two young people become caught up in a thrilling adventure when they are walking through a carriage on a train and suddenly hear a noise that sounds to them like a gun being fired. They rush into the next carriage which is completely empty with its doors swinging backwards and forwards. Then in the restaurant car they ask the first person they meet – who happens to be a waiter – if he also heard the sound.

'No', he says, and goes on to tell them that an old lady is in the carriage – he just saw her going back in there. But when they return, of course, she's gone. Some say the lady never existed but others are sure they saw her. Who's telling the truth, or is everyone on the train lying? Find out at 8 o'clock tonight. It's a brilliant play by Porten and also his last before he moved on to writing for films.

Finally, for those of you who like sailing, *Business Scenes* at 9.30 p.m. brings you the 'unsinkable' boat and a chance to meet its maker, Canadian businessman Peter Field. In 1996, Peter was a manager in a computer company but he left that job to go on a world cruise. He had wanted a stress-free life but ended up back in the rat race, building boats. His new company has many products including luxury boats costing from $1–2 million, which Peter claims will suffer no serious damage even if they hit an iceberg at full speed ... It's all in the type of metal you use, as he explains tonight.

And we also hear about Peter's unusual collection. You would think that a man in his line of work would collect model boats and ships, rather than the old maps which are his real passion! If you tune in this evening, you'll find out how he started his collection and how he hunts for items to add to it!

Well, back to this afternoon's programmes ...

[pause]

Now you'll hear Part Two again.

tone

[The recording is repeated.]

[pause]

That's the end of Part Two.

Now turn to Part Three.

[pause]

PART 3   *You'll hear five different people talking about the way they study. For questions 19 to 23, choose from the list A to F which of the opinions each speaker expresses. Use the letters only once. There is one extra letter which you do not need to use.*

You now have thirty seconds in which to look at Part Three.

[pause]

tone

Speaker 1

Girl: I must say, I've never found it easy to study at home. I've tried all sorts of places. One of my friends prefers to study outside, lying on a rug in the garden.

I try that from time to time and it's nice and airy, though my concentration tends to wander a bit and I find I'm looking at the trees, or people passing by, rather than at my notes. I think better in my bedroom, where it's nice and quiet. I've got a large desk there to put my computer on, and I set my alarm early and work with a fresh mind before everyone else's up.

[pause]

Speaker 2

Boy: You know how sociable I am normally? Well, it's strange but I find people talking really puts me off when I'm trying to study, so I hardly ever work with a classmate, although it's much more fun. You'd think that the faculty library would be the best place for me then – an academic atmosphere and no distractions. You always get a few people whispering and coughing though and that annoys me. What I frequently do instead now is put on my personal stereo and have something blasting away, it doesn't matter what. That blocks out everything else and I get through the work in no time.

[pause]

Speaker 3

Girl: When I do my homework I have to feel right. After sitting on a hard chair all day, I need to stretch out with my head on a pillow. Mum says I cannot possibly concentrate like that, but actually I don't fall asleep as long as I don't go on too late and I have the window open to get some fresh air. I'd love to work with music on, a lot of my friends do, and they say it really helps them concentrate. The point is I like music too much – it takes over from whatever I'm supposed to be doing.

[pause]

Speaker 4

Boy: I'm hopeless at doing school projects. I make timetables so that I can complete the project well before the deadline, but I don't stick to them. I've tried everything – strong coffee, quiet rooms, fresh air. Even though I'm wide awake and there's nothing to disturb me, the work still doesn't get done. I was getting really worried last week, when Mary came round and asked if she could work in my room – hers is too dark and stuffy. I've never worked with a friend before and so I said 'No', but she was desperate. Eventually, I gave in and it really worked out for us both. I couldn't believe it!

[pause]

Speaker 5

Girl: I really like some of the subjects I'm doing this year, particularly maths and physics. I don't mind studying them at all, although some of the homework assignments we're given are quite tricky, so I need to be able to work undisturbed. That's often a bit difficult in our house, unless I put it off until everyone's in bed. Did you know that my younger brother, Fred, plays the guitar in a band? I love some of their music, it's really cool, you'd love it too, but it's pointless trying to work when he's playing.

[pause]

Now you'll hear Part Three again.

tone

[The recording is repeated.]

[pause]

That's the end of Part Three.

Now turn to Part Four.

[pause]

PART 4   *You'll hear a girl called Tricia Simpkins talking at a public meeting about a plan to create a nature reserve in the centre of a large city. For questions 24 to 30, choose the best answer, A, B or C.*

You now have one minute in which to look at Part Four.

[pause]

tone

Man: Good afternoon. Thank you for coming to this public meeting which has been called to discuss the idea of creating a nature reserve in the city – that is, an area where wildlife is protected, and to begin with, local teenager, Tricia Simpkins, is going to tell us some of the background to the idea. Tricia.

Tricia: Yes. Hello ... I'd like to start by saying that, like many city teenagers, I don't have much contact with the countryside. I live off a busy, polluted shopping street, full of people and cars, in the middle of a crowded city and I'd never given any thought to wildlife. Even though every house down my street has got a bit of a garden and we have trees along the road and a piece of waste ground at one end, it seemed nothing out of the ordinary, and I took it all for granted.

My attitude started to change when we had to do a survey of the wildlife in the city as part of a school project. We chose ten families from the street and we asked them just to write down all the animals, birds, insects and so on that they could remember seeing in their garden or down the street during the last couple of years.

All sorts of surprising things soon started coming out of that survey; like that we have twenty different sorts of butterfly, fifty different types of birds, and all sorts of animals, even some quite large ones like foxes and deer. At first we wondered what it meant, like was it a world record or something? We'd no way of knowing. So what we did, we got in touch with a nature reserve out in the country, and asked them what you could see there. And that's when we realised that we've as much, if not more wildlife than they do. And that's what really got us interested in the idea of a nature reserve here.

Because what worries us now is that we may be losing our local wildlife. One specially worrying thing has been all the cutting down of trees in the streets. We've got really big old trees here in this part of the city, and of course if one gets damaged in a storm or gets a disease, it has to be removed. But this year alone, over one hundred of these trees have been chopped down. Now the reason given for this is that the trees have really extensive root systems which makes it difficult for people laying gas pipes, electricity cables and things. But we think these problems are not as serious as they are made out to be, and there's no need for all this destruction.

What's more, although the local council has agreed to plant new trees in place of the old ones, what they're planting are these little ornamental trees that look nice, but the birds and animals just don't use them in the same way. And they're not even saving money, because more suitable trees cost just the same.

Another example of what can happen is the wasteland at the end of our street. It belongs to the city council and as children we all used to play there and we thought it was really great because it was so covered in bushes and wild flowers that you could get lost if you went off the little muddy tracks. Then, a few years ago, no doubt thinking they were doing the right thing, the council decided to tidy it up. Now it's just an area of grass where people go to exercise their dogs. There are a few little trees, but basically there's not a lot there any more.

So, what I'd like to propose this afternoon is that we use this space to create a nature reserve. We think it should be allowed to go back to its natural condition, thus providing a refuge for the local wildlife which may be suffering from the loss of trees in the area. This would, of course, also be a leisure amenity for people who want to get away from the stresses of city living, which is hardly something we would want to deny them.

So, I would like you ...

[pause]

Now you'll hear Part Four again.

tone

[The recording is repeated.]

[pause]

That's the end of Part Four.

There'll now be a pause of five minutes for you to copy your answers onto the separate answer sheet. Be sure to follow the numbering of all the questions. I'll remind you when there is one minute left, so that you are sure to finish in time.

[Teacher, pause the recording here for five minutes. Remind your students when they have one minute left.]

That's the end of the test. Please stop now. Your supervisor will now collect all the question papers and answer sheets.

Test 3 Key

Paper 1 Reading (1 hour)

Part 1

1 B   2 C   3 A   4 C   5 B   6 A   7 D   8 C

Part 2

9 E   10 G   11 B   12 H   13 C   14 F   15 D

Part 3

16 B   17 A or E   18 A or E   19 B   20 C   21 E   22 C or D
23 C or D   24 A   25 C   26 D   27 B   28 A or E
29 A or E   30 D

Paper 2 Writing (1 hour 20 minutes)

Task-specific Mark Schemes

Part 1

Question 1

Content
The letter should include all the points in the notes:
1) express enthusiasm about idea of making a short film
2) say which month would be best and why
3) give Ben details of an interesting place to visit
4) offer to show the group around the town.

Organisation and cohesion
Clear organisation of ideas, with suitable paragraphing, linking and opening/closing formulae as appropriate to the task.

Range
Language relating to the functions above.
Vocabulary relating to visit and arrangements.

Appropriacy of register and format
Standard English appropriate to the situation and target reader, observing grammar and spelling conventions.

Target reader
Would be informed.

Part 2

Question 2

Content
The letter should give details relevant to the advertised job.

Organisation and cohesion
Clear organisation of ideas, with suitable paragraphing and linking with suitable opening and closing formulae.

Range
Language of explanation and description.
Vocabulary relating to music, work experience and language ability.

Appropriacy of register and format
Consistent register suitable to the situation and target reader.

Target reader
Would be informed.

Question 3

Content
The story should continue from the prompt sentence.

Organisation and cohesion
Storyline should be clear. Paragraphing could be minimal.

Range
Narrative tenses. Vocabulary appropriate to the chosen topic of story.

Appropriacy of register and format
Consistent register suitable to the story.

Target reader
Would be able to follow the storyline.

Question 4

Content
The article should describe the holiday destination and say why it is special.

Organisation and cohesion
Clear organisation of ideas, with suitable paragraphing and linking.

Range
Language of description, explanation and opinion.
Vocabulary relating to chosen location.

Appropriacy of register and format
Consistent register suitable to the situation and target reader.

Target reader
Would be informed.

Question 5(a)

Content
The essay should agree or disagree with the statement.

Organisation and cohesion
Clear organisation of ideas, with suitable paragraphing and linking.

Range
Language of explanation, description and opinion.
Vocabulary relating to describing character and situation.

Appropriacy of register and format
Consistent register suitable to the situation and target reader.

Target reader
Would be informed.

Question 5(b)

Content
The essay should describe one mistake which Passepartout makes during the journey.

Organisation and cohesion
Clear organisation of ideas, with suitable paragraphing and linking.

Range
Language of description and explanation.
Vocabulary relating to the incident being described.

Appropriacy of register and format
Consistent register suitable to the situation and target reader.

Target reader
Would be informed.

Paper 3 Use of English (45 minutes)

Part 1

1 D   2 B   3 B   4 D   5 A   6 C   7 B   8 A   9 B   10 C
11 D   12 C

Part 2

13 have / need / ought   14 If   15 how   16 of   17 getting / making / having
18 more   19 On   20 into   21 take   22 like   23 sure / certain   24 rather

Part 3

25 coastal   26 unevenly   27 economic   28 growth   29 arrivals
30 employment   31 concentration   32 remarkable   33 industrial   34 expansion

Part 4

35 had/'d got/gotten/been | in **touch** with **36** no (possible) **comparison** (at all) | between
37 what | **made** Sarah/her leave **38** taking **care** | of **39** nobody / no-one / none of us |
came up **40** did not / didn't / refused to / would not / wouldn't | **let** her **41** would
have/'ve **turned** up | on **42** were **prevented** | from getting

Paper 4 Listening (approximately 40 minutes)

Part 1

1 B **2** A **3** C **4** C **5** C **6** B **7** B **8** B

Part 2

9 woodwork **10** detective **11** (old) photos/photographs **12** theatre/theater
13 Japan (and) Canada *IN EITHER ORDER* **14** (an) electric light / (a) light / (electric)
lighting/lights **15** 140 cm(s) / one hundred (and) forty centimetres/centimeters
16 windows **17** paper **18** (of) (the) pollution

Part 3

19 D **20** B **21** E **22** C **23** A

Part 4

24 C **25** C **26** B **27** A **28** A **29** B **30** C

Transcript *This is the Cambridge First Certificate in English Listening Test. Test Three.*

I'm going to give you the instructions for this test.
I'll introduce each part of the test and give you time to look at the questions.
At the start of each piece you'll hear this sound:

tone

You'll hear each piece twice.

Remember, while you're listening, write your answers on the question paper.
You'll have five minutes at the end of the test to copy your answers onto the
separate answer sheet.

There will now be a pause. Please ask any questions now, because you must
not speak during the test.

[pause]

Now open your question paper and look at Part One.

[pause]

PART 1 *You'll hear people talking in eight different situations. For questions 1 to 8,*
choose the best answer, A, B or C.

Question 1	One. *You hear some information about a country on a travel programme.* *Where do most people spend the summer months?* A *at the seaside* B *in the capital city* C *in the mountains* [pause] tone In the main summer months, the weather in the capital city is hot and the humidity is terrible. If you're there then, the best thing to do is either sit in a pool all day or surround yourself with air-conditioning. You could, however, head higher where it's cooler. The Citra Mountains behind the north-east coast have stunning scenery, but the majority never seem to make the effort to get out of the capital, which is a pity because the coast and the mountains are much pleasanter. [pause] tone [The recording is repeated.] [pause]
Question 2	Two. *You hear part of a radio programme about chewing gum.* *What is the speaker doing?* A *outlining its history* B *describing why it has changed* C *explaining its popularity* [pause] tone Although it's popular worldwide, chewing gum is a uniquely US product, discovered during the search for rubber materials in the 1860s. The basic raw material for all chewing gum is the natural gum, chicle, obtained from the sapodilla tree found in Central America. Recently, man-made substitutes have come into widespread use and popular types of chewing gum now include a soft-chunk bubble gum and a gum filled with flavoured liquid. In the US alone, sales of chewing gum total over $800 million a year, and worldwide some several billion. [pause] tone [The recording is repeated.] [pause]

Question 3	*Three.* *You hear part of a radio programme where listeners phone in with their* *opinions.* *What does the man want to do?* *A express his disappointment* *B complain about his situation* *C encourage other listeners*

[pause]

tone

Woman:	Go ahead, David. What have you got to say?
Man:	Well, I'm 55. I was a bank manager until ten years ago, and then I lost my job. I was angry, I can tell you. But you can't just sit about feeling sorry for yourself – like most of your callers. Can I just say to anyone listening: my story will give you heart. A bank manager has to be a good listener, right? So I thought, 'How can I use that skill?' – maybe I could be a counsellor of some sort – you know, help people deal with their personal problems. I'm busier now than I've ever been!

[pause]

tone

[The recording is repeated.]

[pause]

Question 4	*Four.* *You hear a woman speaking on the radio about buying a painting for the* *first time.* *What opinion is she expressing?* *A A painting can be a worthwhile investment.* *B Only buy a painting if you have room for it.* *C Take your time when buying your first painting.*

[pause]

tone

The first rule about buying a painting is to immediately put aside any notion that this will make you enough money to keep you in your old age. The overriding factor is that you must really like the work itself. Ask yourself, can you imagine it on the wall next to the TV? Are you happy to have this painting as a fixture in your life? With this in mind, you can now set about looking into the art market. You should do your homework. Fine tune your taste; visit a student exhibition; flick through some contemporary art magazines.

[pause]

tone

[The recording is repeated.]

[pause]

Question 5	*Five.*
	You hear a man being interviewed on the radio.
	What does he say about his mother?
	A She helped him become an artist.
	B She persuaded him to do research.
	C She wanted him to make money.

[pause]

tone

My mother could see I was artistic and she would never have stood in my way, but she was desperate to ensure that I would do well in life, financially I mean, as she had always struggled. So she helped me with my science homework – she really pushed me – if it hadn't been for her, I wouldn't be where I am today. I feel, deep down, I do have a more natural talent for art, rather than science; I even won some awards for my pictures ... and I still paint whenever I can. But I suppose, when I was growing up, I didn't think I would ever earn enough as an artist, so I studied science at university, then spent a few years in the States working as a researcher in the oil industry.

[pause]

tone

[The recording is repeated.]

[pause]

Question 6	*Six.*
	You hear part of an interview with a woman who is talking about her day.
	What is her profession?
	A a teacher
	B a doctor
	C a farmer

[pause]

tone

My day starts at 6 o'clock – it's somewhat chaotic at home early in the morning as we're all rushing around! I try to help my husband feed the animals, and then there's the twins to get ready for school, and I get to the surgery at around 8 a.m. There's always a lot of paperwork to do. Then it's seeing patients all day. We've got a trainee watching us at the moment for six months, so I spend some time with her, making sure she's making sense of it all – I enjoy working with students.

[pause]

tone

[The recording is repeated.]

[pause]

Question 7   *Seven.*
You hear a man talking on the radio about teaching beginners to surf in the sea.
What does the man say about beginners?
A They are very sensitive to criticism.
B They need to be given appropriate goals.
C They often start off with the wrong attitude.

[pause]

tone

When you teach beginners, in a sense you have to tailor-make a course for each of them – getting the objectives right for each day's course is fundamental – age or sex makes little difference, it's attitude. Some are delighted if they manage to get their knees on a surfboard, or maybe standing up in the first session is enough. Most can learn to stand up in half a day because of the foamy boards we use. Others just keep going until they've succeeded. Some make daft mistakes like putting their arms through the legs of their wetsuits, but most beginners are quite sensible!

[pause]

tone

[The recording is repeated.]

[pause]

Question 8   *Eight.*
You hear part of an interview with a crime novelist.
What point is he making about his novels?
A They are based on real-life crimes.
B They include accurate descriptions of life in the past.
C They vary in length depending on the historical period.

[pause]

tone

Interviewer: Now John, you write around four historical crime novels each year. How do you manage it?
John: Well, although the characters and stories themselves are made up, I want my books to be historically correct in the details of everyday life I describe. And the further back in history you go, the fewer actual details survive. So, I'm careful to keep them to a similar length, and then I'm less tempted to invent things. And, let's face it, if a detective takes more than 80,000 words to solve a crime, he begins to look a bit dim, doesn't he?

[pause]

tone

[The recording is repeated.]

[pause]

[pause]

PART 2   *You will hear a man called Peter Welby, who makes small models of buildings, talking about his work. For questions 9 to 18, complete the sentences.*

You now have forty-five seconds in which to look at Part Two.

[pause]

tone

My job is model-making. I make small copies of large buildings and other structures. It might seem a strange job, but I knew when I was at school that it was what I wanted to do. So I did a college course, not in art or architecture as you might expect, but in woodwork. Because of the concentration on fine detail it requires, it was ideal for a model-maker. Although later, of course, I had to adapt my skills to other materials as well. When I make a model of an old building, often original parts of the building have been damaged or even completely demolished over the years, so I have to work hard to find out what they must have been like. Actually, I think there's quite a lot in common between what I do and what a detective does ... tracking down clues, working things out ...

   I've done quite a few jobs now. The toughest commission I've ever had was from Ireland. I was asked to do a model of part of a large house which had burnt down years before. They just gave me a few old photos to use, as there was no actual building to copy. I've done all sorts of buildings since, everything from grand castles to the most ordinary farmhouse. The one I liked most, though, was where I had to rebuild a theatre. The original building was gone, but this time there were detailed drawings to work from. My model was then shown in an exhibition called 'All the World's a Stage' here in London. It was fun because I could go and look at it every day if I wanted to; see how people were reacting to it. Generally, though, I don't see my models again after I've delivered them, as 80% of them are shipped out to Japan or Canada, with the rest shared between England and France. I do try to give pretty careful instructions, however, about how the models should be displayed. The height at which they should stand, how large the space around them should be, and also about lighting, because the colours and details come out most clearly if there's electric light directly above them. Daylight's too pale.

   And that's particularly true of my most recent project, a model of a very interesting old building called Marney House. The owners decided to open it to the public and wanted a model to display for visitors. The detail work was very challenging indeed, as I had to reduce the original to a model just one hundred and forty centimetres high, which is seventy-six times smaller than the real building ... that's *small*, yet everything has to be there. It actually took longer than any model I've ever done before, mainly because I had to do all of the 150 windows ... a real test of patience! There were times, to be honest, when I found myself regretting the fact that I'd ever taken the project on in the first place. On top of that, I had to make every single one of the thousands of roof tiles individually out of paper. Mind you, when I had finished that process, I knew the hardest part was over, and that the rest would be quite fun. Doing things like the statues along the front was enjoyable, because every one's different ... and I spent some happy hours playing around with colours to get the exact reproduction of the original interior walls. When I'd finished all that, the only remaining problem was that, of course, the whole thing looked like a model of a new building. So I did what I usually do, which is to carefully wash the outside of the model with watercolour, so that it looks as if, over the years, it's been affected by wind and rain, and also pollution, of course. The owners were very pleased with the result, and I'm glad I can go and see it from time to time. Model-making is a great job, and I'd recommend it to anyone with patience and an eye for detail.

[pause]

Now you'll hear Part Two again.

tone

[The recording is repeated.]

[pause]

That's the end of Part Two.

Now turn to Part Three.

[pause]

PART 3   *You'll hear five different people talking about hotels they have recently stayed in with their children. For questions 19 to 23, choose from the list A to F what each speaker says. Use the letters only once. There is one extra letter which you do not need to use.*

You now have thirty seconds in which to look at Part Three.

[pause]

tone

Speaker 1

Woman: We chose this hotel because we knew that the owners had young children of their own. The room could have been a bit bigger, but then it was quite inexpensive. They provided an early supper if you told them in good time, so that the parents could eat in peace later in the cosy dining room. There were hundreds of toys for the children to play with, a huge garden with a playground, ponds and a playhouse. We hardly saw our two all week.

[pause]

Speaker 2

Man: We always have difficulty finding hotels which welcome our children. This one was particularly good because the bedroom had a separate sitting room so we

153

weren't all squashed together in one room. Although it wasn't the cheapest around, far from it in fact, it was worth it. Our teenage kids loved the outdoor heated swimming pool and the mountain bikes, which were provided free by the hotel. Apparently, the owners' kids, who've grown up and left home now, had been mad on mountain biking. There was also an all-weather tennis court. Another thing we liked was the separate dining room for people with young families.

[pause]

Speaker 3

Woman: We'd had a bad experience the year before at a hotel which didn't cater for children. But this year we were very impressed by the hospitality of the hotel. The rooms were large enough to accommodate four beds comfortably and there was an adventure playground in the garden for the younger kids. You don't have to pay for children under ten sharing the room – even meals were free for them, so that was another bonus. There was lots to do including horse riding and tennis. But if you wanted to swim you had to go to the local leisure centre, which the kids loved.

[pause]

Speaker 4

Man: In the hotel we went to, we had a family suite which was very spacious. There was an outdoor heated pool and large grounds so the kids spent most of the time in the pool. So long as your children like swimming you're alright 'cos there wasn't much else for them to do. I did think that they could have put in a playground too. Young children under ten aren't allowed in the dining room but there was an early supper for them. This meant that we could have a quiet dinner for two when they were in bed.

[pause]

Speaker 5

Woman: What we liked about our hotel was its size. It was only a small hotel and we were looked after like family. The room had loads of soft toys, wooden toys and books, which the children loved. The guest lounge and conservatory was a child-free zone after seven thirty which suited us fine 'cos there was a special children's supper at six, which meant that they could go to bed early and get a good night's sleep. Older children aren't really catered for and this hotel is probably better for those with younger kids.

[pause]

Now you'll hear Part Three again.

tone

[The recording is repeated.]

[pause]

That's the end of Part Three.

Now turn to Part Four.

[pause]

PART 4   *You'll hear a radio interview with a young tennis player, Alice Winters, and her coach, Bruce Gray. For questions 24 to 30, choose the best answer, A, B or C.*

You now have one minute in which to look at Part Four.

[pause]

tone

Presenter:	In some sports, the players seem to be getting younger and younger. My guests today are 14-year-old Alice Winters and her coach, Bruce Gray. Alice, as National Junior Tennis Champion, has been described as 'the most talented young player for years'. Alice, Bruce, welcome.
Alice/Bruce:	Hello.
Presenter:	Let's start by talking about money. Have you found it easy to get help in that respect, Bruce?
Bruce:	Not really. We've applied to local companies for sponsorship but they would sooner put their money into something which gets them publicity – Alice isn't *that* well known yet. So we'll probably have to get there without it, and I reckon that, with Alice's talent, there's no reason why we can't. That'd be an even greater achievement, wouldn't it?
Presenter:	Now Alice, you must do a lot of training? Is it sometimes a bit too demanding for someone of your age?
Alice:	Well, a lot of players my age might ask themselves, 'Why can't I be like everyone else?', you know, free in the evenings and at weekends, but that side of it doesn't bother me. I must admit though that there are times when I just don't fancy it – you know, freezing cold winter mornings when Bruce comes round to take me on a training run and I think, 'Oh go away and leave me alone!' But apart from that, well, I do it because I enjoy it. Nobody's making me do it, are they? So I don't really see it as making sacrifices.
Presenter:	And what about your schoolwork?
Alice:	Well, I'm managing to keep up with that at the moment, although I can see that if I do get more successful the sport might get in the way of academic work, but, well, I know which comes first for me. After all, if I make it to the top in tennis, I won't need any academic qualifications.
Presenter:	Now Alice, when you're competing in a tournament, is it all terribly serious or do you have fun?
Alice:	Well, I'm only there for one reason really. I mean, I can't see the point otherwise. I'm not one of those people who think that taking part matters more than winning. I mean, I know I can't win every time, especially up against people a lot older than me, but that's always the aim. And if I lose, well, I look at my performance with Bruce, look at ways of improving it, and well, I don't let it get to me. I'm just more determined next time.
Presenter:	Bruce, what do you think makes Alice different from other players of the same age?

Bruce:	I've never come across any young player quite like her in all my years as a coach. What amazes me is – you can watch her play and she doesn't seem to be trying, even though of course she is. With other players you can see the effort involved but with her, well, she's just so gifted.
Presenter:	So Alice, how do you see your future?
Alice:	Well, I'd love to turn professional, but it's a bit early to think seriously about that. I mean, I'm a big fish in a small pond at the moment, but as I get older, well, there are going to be a lot of tough players out there. If I do end up doing it full time ... the lifestyle looks glamorous from outside, but it might just be too hard for me and I might decide to get out. But it's hard to say. Some people stay at the top for years, don't they?
Presenter:	Bruce, do you and Alice get on well? Is she an easy person to coach?
Bruce:	You know, sometimes I find it difficult to remember how young she is because she's got an old head on young shoulders. We've had the odd ... shall I say ... disagreement but she doesn't have much of a temper, it soon passes. She doesn't have a great deal to say, I guess, when we're working or travelling to tournaments. She has friends outside the game, but she doesn't have much time for a social life at the moment.
Presenter:	Well, Alice and Bruce, thanks for being my guests and good luck for the future.
Alice/Bruce:	Thank you.

[pause]

Now you'll hear Part Four again.

tone

[The recording is repeated.]

[pause]

That's the end of Part Four.

There'll now be a pause of five minutes for you to copy your answers onto the separate answer sheet. Be sure to follow the numbering of all the questions. I'll remind you when there is one minute left, so that you are sure to finish in time.

[Teacher, pause the recording here for five minutes. Remind your students when they have one minute left.]

That's the end of the test. Please stop now. Your supervisor will now collect all the question papers and answer sheets.

Test 4 Key

Paper 1   Reading (1 hour)

Part 1

1 B   2 D   3 A   4 C   5 C   6 A   7 D   8 B

Part 2

9 H   10 A   11 C   12 F   13 B   14 D   15 G

Part 3

16 B   17 A   18 C   19 D   20 E   21 A   22 E   23 D   24 E
25 D   26 B   27 F   28 C   29 E   30 A

Paper 2   Writing (1 hour 20 minutes)

Task-specific Mark Schemes

Part 1

Question 1

Content
The email should include all the points in the notes:
1) accept invitation to visit in July
2) give Pat ideas for birthday present
3) say that camping is not a good idea
4) ask for additional information.

Organisation and cohesion
Clear organisation of ideas, with suitable paragraphing, linking and opening/closing formulae as appropriate to the task.

Range
Language relating to the functions above.
Vocabulary relating to invitation and arrangements.

Appropriacy of register and format
Standard English appropriate to the situation and target reader observing grammar and spelling conventions.

Target reader
Would be informed.

Part 2
Question 2
Content
The essay should give opinion on the statement.

Organisation and cohesion
Clear organisation of ideas with suitable paragraphing and linking.

Range
Language of describing, explaining and expressing opinion.
Vocabulary relating to environment.

Appropriacy of register and format
Consistent register suitable to the situation and target reader.

Target reader
Would be informed.

Question 3
Content
The article should describe preferred method of travel.

Organisation and cohesion
Clear organisation of ideas, with suitable paragraphing and linking.

Range
Language of explanation and opinion.
Vocabulary relating to travel and transport.

Appropriacy of register and format
Consistent register suitable to the situation and target reader.

Target reader
Would be informed.

Question 4
Content
The report should give details of local food specialities and eating habits.

Organisation and cohesion
Clear organisation of ideas, with suitable paragraphing and linking. Headings an advantage but not essential.

Range
Language of description and explanation.
Vocabulary relating to food and eating habits.

Appropriacy of register and format
Consistent register suitable to the situation and target reader.

Target reader
Would be informed.

Question 5(a)

Content
The letter should give information about unpleasant character in *The Citadel*.

Organisation and cohesion
Clear organisation of ideas, with suitable paragraphing and linking.

Range
Language of description and opinion.
Vocabulary relating to character chosen.

Appropriacy of register and format
Consistent register suitable to the situation and target reader.

Target reader
Would be informed.

Question 5(b)

Content
The essay should give information on the character chosen.

Organisation and cohesion
Clear organisation of ideas, with suitable paragraphing and linking.

Range
Language of description and opinion.
Vocabulary relating to describing people.

Appropriacy of register and format
Consistent register suitable to the situation and target reader.

Target reader
Would be informed.

Paper 3 Use of English (45 minutes)

Part 1

1 B   2 D   3 A   4 C   5 B   6 D   7 C   8 C   9 D   10 A
11 A   12 B

Part 2

13 have   14 taking   15 which / that   16 after   17 a   18 such
19 Although / Though / While / Whilst   20 much   21 are   22 full   23 was
24 more

Part 3

25 reminder   26 importance   27 punctually   28 anxious   29 ability
30 recommendation   31 anger   32 unusual   33 appearance   34 reliable

Part 4

35 been | **put** off/back   36 car was **being** | driven   37 **before** anybody/anyone | said
38 carried on | getting up   39 would/'d **rather** | eat/have   40 apologised/apologized
for | (his) behaving / having behaved OR **apologised/apologized** because | he had behaved
41 **possible** for | Jenny/her to get/arrive/reach   42 no **point** (in) | (us/our) leaving

Paper 4   Listening (approximately 40 minutes)

Part 1

1 B   2 C   3 A   4 A   5 A   6 B   7 B   8 B

Part 2

9 composer   10 concert halls / concerts   11 9500 / nine and a half thousand / nine
thousand five hundred   12 contacts   13 mending   14 wood   15 school /
schoolroom   16 (small) museum   17 heating (bill(s))   18 dry

Part 3

19 C   20 E   21 A   22 F   23 D

Part 4

24 C   25 A   26 B   27 B   28 C   29 B   30 C

Transcript   *This is the Cambridge First Certificate in English Listening Test. Test Four.*

I'm going to give you the instructions for this test.
I'll introduce each part of the test and give you time to look at the questions.
At the start of each piece you'll hear this sound:

tone

You'll hear each piece twice.

Remember, while you're listening, write your answers on the question paper.
You'll have five minutes at the end of the test to copy your answers onto the
separate answer sheet.

There will now be a pause. Please ask any questions now, because you must
not speak during the test.

[pause]

Now open your question paper and look at Part One.

[pause]

PART 1   *You'll hear people talking in eight different situations. For questions 1 to 8, choose the best answer, A, B or C.*

Question 1   *One.*
You hear someone talking about women's football.
What is she doing when she speaks?
A encouraging young girls to support a team
B suggesting how to attract young girls to the sport
C asking young girls to take the sport seriously

[pause]

tone

I think we really have to encourage young girls to get involved in women's football, to show them it's a great sport and there are opportunities to play on the world stage, things like the women's World Cup, things like the Olympic Games. That's what inspires young kids to do things. They get to see role models and they get to see opportunities for them to perform, you know, in front of huge audiences. So, I think if we want this sport to develop, this is the message we have to get across.

[pause]

tone

[The recording is repeated.]

[pause]

Question 2   *Two.*
You hear a man talking on the radio about a bag made for use on walking trips.
How does this new bag differ from others?
A It has pockets on the side.
B You can take off the rain cover.
C There are some extra features.

[pause]

tone

This model from Vango's impressive range is one of those bags that you can use quite happily on long walking trips. It has well-made, comfortable straps, large side pockets and, as on their bigger bags, there is a removable rain cover – very useful in this changeable climate. Interestingly, they've added an internal pocket for a water flask and a key clip, both of which make this bag excellent value compared to other models available.

[pause]

tone

[The recording is repeated.]

[pause]

Question 3

Three.
On the radio, you hear a man discussing a cartoon film about dinosaurs.
What aspect of the film disappointed him?
A the design of the backgrounds
B the quality of the sound effects
C the size of the dinosaurs

[pause]

tone

Well, it's an amazing film. They got all the details right, well, almost. They certainly give you a good idea of just how enormous these creatures were, they make you feel really tiny ... and the way they move is so believable ... Having said that, I feel there should have been more research into the scenic effects, you need to know what their environment was like, the kinds of plants these giants were eating ... What they had was some kind of strange landscape ... But, when it came to the noises that these beasts would have made, you were left in no doubt, a lot of effort had gone into making them terrifyingly realistic ...

[pause]

tone

[The recording is repeated.]

[pause]

Question 4

Four.
You overhear a couple talking about keeping fit.
What do they agree about?
A the need to be more active
B the benefits of joining a gym
C the dangers of too much exercise

[pause]

tone

Woman: We ought to take more exercise, you know.
Man: Well, there's probably something in that, but I resent constantly being told by the media that I'm not active enough.
Woman: Well, doctors want people to take that message on board too.
Man: So people join a gym, spend a fortune on fitness videos, then within a few weeks get fed up with it, so it's money down the drain.

Woman:	Some people manage to keep it up.
Man:	Yes, and then they start overdoing it, so that it rules their life.
Woman:	I don't think there's much danger of that in your case.

[pause]

tone

[The recording is repeated.]

[pause]

Question 5

Five.
In a radio play, you hear a woman talking on the phone to a friend.
Where does the woman want her friend to meet her?
A on the beach
B at the bank
C in a shop

[pause]

tone

Hi, glad I caught you in. I'm phoning from my mobile, and guess where I am now? ... Yeah, can you hear the waves? Tell you what, we can both do the shopping together this evening if you like, it won't take long. How about coming to join me for a couple of hours first? ... No, I've got enough cash, I went past the bank this morning, but if you need some, get it on your way here. OK, so is that settled then? See you soon, I promise you won't regret it!

[pause]

tone

[The recording is repeated.]

[pause]

Question 6

Six.
You hear a student talking to his friend about a meeting with his tutor.
What was the student's purpose in meeting his tutor?
A to see if there was a part-time job available
B to ask for financial assistance
C to request more time to complete coursework

[pause]

tone

Woman:	How did it go then?
Man:	Well, I didn't say what I wanted immediately. First we talked about the difficulty of the course and how much pressure it puts on students and so on. I mean last month I had to ask for an extension on both my assignments.

Woman:	Mmm. I did too. You're not alone there. And?
Man:	I finally got to the point saying I'd lost my part-time job and had money problems. She mentioned that there were special grants for those having difficulty with the costs. So I got an application form to fill in and if they accept that, it'll cover the fees for the next six months, so problem solved.
Woman:	Great.

[pause]

tone

[The recording is repeated.]

[pause]

Question 7
Seven.
You hear a man talking about learning how to paint landscapes.
What does he say about it?
A It proved easier than he had thought.
B It showed him he had some talent.
C It opened up opportunities for him.

[pause]

tone

The best way to learn how to paint is out in the open, with a teacher giving you guidance. Sitting on a stool and painting, you forget about everything else. I thought it would be demanding, and it was, although I wasn't trying to become a professional. Choosing and mixing the colours, trying to create perfect clouds ... I was amazed when people passed by and peered over my shoulder and said, 'I wish I could do that!' Seeing artists at work had always fascinated me, but at school a teacher's report had said: 'Peter has no feeling for art or design.' Then at last I knew she'd been wrong.

[pause]

tone

[The recording is repeated.]

[pause]

Question 8
Eight.
You turn on the radio and hear a man talking.
What is he talking about?
A finding friendship
B solving problems
C helping others

[pause]

tone

It's sometimes hard to deal with a difficult situation on your own. Having the support of someone else can make all the difference and we should recognise that getting the aid of a friend or relative is a strength and not a weakness. So often we are led to believe that sharing our challenges is a sign of failure. This simply isn't true. The most successful people are those who know how and when to ask for help so don't battle on with things on your own if you don't need to. Here are a few tips on how to …

[pause]

tone

[The recording is repeated.]

[pause]

That's the end of Part One.

Now turn to Part Two.

[pause]

PART 2   *You will hear an interview with a man called Richard Porter who is a maker of musical instruments called organs. For questions 9 to 18, complete the sentences.*

You now have forty-five seconds in which to look at Part Two.

[pause]

tone

Interviewer: Good evening and welcome to the programme where, as you know, we go out and talk to people who run their own companies. Today, we're talking to Richard Porter, who makes large concert organs as a profession. Richard, tell us, just how did you get into this area of work?

Richard: Well, I play the piano and, as a child, I had a good teacher who wrote her own music, and I always wanted to be a composer too. However, my parents persuaded me that what I needed to do was go to college and study how to make musical instruments, rather than play them, because they saw more of a future in that. And now, I make the organs which are played in churches and concert halls all around the world. The one thing that I never intended to do was become a businessman, which is what I am now really, as well as being an instrument maker.

Interviewer: So, when did you start making organs?

Richard: About five years ago. I started from a room in my house, but now I have my own workshop.

Interviewer: So, it must pay.

Richard: Well, an organ sells at £9500, which means around £3500 profit for me I suppose.

Interviewer: And how long does it take to build one?

Richard: It might take me three months to complete one, and when I say three months, I mean three months of working seventy hours a week. Although that sounds a lot, I have to say I don't mind because I love the work and I get to meet lots of interesting people. Most of my commissions are from overseas clients and they're nearly all the result of personal contacts. I rarely use advertising these days.

Interviewer: So, you make a living out of it?

Richard: Not really. The most profitable part of my business is actually mending organs, generally old large ones so they can be used for concerts and recording sessions. That can earn me up to £300 each time. Which is just as well, because I do need to have money available to buy the raw materials for the larger organs. There's a lot of investment to make before I can start to build. I get the wood from Britain, but most of the other components come from France or Germany.

Interviewer: And I understand you've made a big decision recently?

Richard: Yes. I've decided to take the opportunity to move my workshop to a former schoolroom that has become available in Lincolnshire, about a hundred miles away.

Interviewer: So, you're moving house as well?

Richard: Yes. We're moving there in three months' time.

Interviewer: Tell me about the new workshop.

Richard: It is a lovely old building attached to the Town Hall in a small market town. In return for using the workshop, I've agreed to spend forty days a year working as a museum attendant. There's a small museum in the town that has visiting exhibitions, but is only open on certain days in the year.

Interviewer: And is that something you're looking forward to?

Richard: Not really, but it means that I save around £4000 a year because apart from paying the heating bill the workshop is rent free. That's the great thing about the place. It's also very close to our new house, so I'll have the luxury of walking to work each morning, which is nice.

Interviewer: Is it easy to find a building that is suitable as a workshop?

Richard: No it isn't. It's very easy for the instruments to get damaged so the environment must be dry. None of the buildings I've worked in so far have been dry enough. The new workshop is perfect in that respect.

Interviewer: Oh right. Well, best of luck to you in that new project. Now, I think you're going to play us a piece on an organ which you built yourself ...

[pause]

Now you'll hear Part Two again.

tone

[The recording is repeated.]

[pause]

That's the end of Part Two.

Now turn to Part Three.

[pause]

PART 3   *You'll hear five different cyclists talking about a long-distance race they took part in. For questions 19 to 23, choose from the list A to F, what each speaker says. Use the letters only once. There is one extra letter which you do not need to use.*

You now have thirty seconds in which to look at Part Three.

[pause]

tone

Speaker 1

[pause]

Woman: This was my first bike ride across the really difficult ground. When you ride at speed on rough tracks, it's hard to find an easy riding position, and as a result you get an unpleasant stiffness in your back. You can stand up on the bike, and that sometimes helps. But it didn't with me. On the contrary, I found myself flying over the handle bars a couple of times, landing on soft grass, luckily. If the bike had been damaged I'd have stopped then and there, but it was OK. I carried on to the end but the slight pain in my back didn't get any better.

[pause]

Speaker 2

[pause]

Man: We cycled through towns and also through remote areas, and everything was fine until I came to a hilly bit. I knew I had an advantage here, because I'm good at speeding up slopes. No aching muscles for me! But at some point during the climb, I noticed one of the wheels needed adjusting. I'd been told before the start that there'd be a support team, so even if your bike broke down they'd be there to help you immediately. Well, they certainly weren't capable of running things properly because I had to wait far too long, and so was one of the last competitors to reach the finishing line.

[pause]

Speaker 3

[pause]

Man: I'd been involved in all the planning stages of the race, and so it seemed a good idea to take part. However, halfway through, I realised my best option was to turn back. I hadn't done enough training. In a race like that, you need to keep a regular speed, even when you are going up what looks like a mountainside. If you are not fit enough, your leg muscles may seem to refuse to keep on pedalling hard! I saw other riders speeding past me – I couldn't believe it. Anyway, I thought, this is silly, I may end up with a torn muscle, so that was that.

[pause]

Speaker 4

[pause]

Woman: Well, I think I was just plain unlucky. I came up this village road and there were all these cars moving slowly uphill. There had been an accident or something. Anyway, it was impossible to overtake them, on such a narrow path, so they slowed me down. I'm content with what I've achieved, although I didn't win any of the prizes. Basically, I managed all the difficult bits of the race, and I know that if it hadn't been for that problem, I would have had a good chance of winning. Also my bike was great, I'd had it repaired recently and wasn't sure it would stand this test.

[pause]

Speaker 5

[pause]

Man: I have lots of cycling experience, but I knew this was going to be a long race, and your muscles can get very tired and strained. But I was ready for the challenge, after months of weightlifting to increase my strength. In fact, I could almost say I overdid it, because I developed an elbow problem a couple of months before the race, which fortunately was not serious. But I certainly wasn't expecting my bike to give me any trouble! But that's what happened, unfortunately. I had started the race feeling fitter than ever, so it was all the more disappointing that it had to end like this.

[pause]

Now you'll hear Part Three again.

tone

[The recording is repeated.]

[pause]

That's the end of Part Three.

Now turn to Part Four.

[pause]

PART 4   *You'll hear an interview with a TV presenter, Tanya Edwards, who is talking about her career and her daughter called Maddy. For questions 24 to 30, choose the best answer, A, B or C.*

You now have one minute in which to look at Part Four.

[pause]

tone

Interviewer:	Today, in our series about celebrity families, the TV presenter Tanya Edwards talks about her first job and also about her daughter, Maddy, a pop star and model. Tanya, your first job was in children's television, wasn't it?
Tanya:	When I was asked to audition for a job presenting on children's television, I didn't want to do the job at all. I'd always wanted to be an actress, and had done a lot of acting at college. In fact, it was the closest thing to acting that I could possibly have chosen, because it was presenting a live programme – so having been on stage in college productions came in handy. In those days, we didn't have talkback – you know, that's where you have a little gadget stuck in your ear, and you can hear the producer talking to you – so we had to rely on signals from the floor manager … which worked fine.
Interviewer:	You had an extraordinary boss, didn't you?
Tanya:	Yes. Paul Broadly. He was a very well-respected programme editor. He taught me so much. He seemed quite old to me when I started – he was a grandfather – but he had this way of understanding what children could enjoy watching. He was absolutely determined to produce the best children's television – whether it was something about wildlife on safari, or how to make a chocolate cake. He was devoted to the programme, completely single-minded about it, and expected us to feel exactly the same.
Interviewer:	But you enjoyed it?
Tanya:	Oh yes, and there was always something different. I even did parachuting for the programme. There I was, leaping out of this aeroplane, with the cameras on me – trying to smile, although it was pretty scary! The stupid thing was that the jump went fine, but I fell over running back to the car, carrying the parachute – and broke my ankle. I thought my boss would be furious, but in fact he was okay about it, and I was amazed that lots of the children who watched the programme sent me cards – one even sent me a cake.
Interviewer:	And your daughter is Maddy, the singer and model. Did she always want to be famous?
Tanya:	Well, we always had a lot of music in the house, when she was young. I wouldn't say that I knew that she would do something special – I had to persuade her to learn an instrument – but I do remember one day, she was supposed to be doing her homework, and my husband came down the road and there was Maddy leaning out of the window, playing her flute for all she was worth. It was a nice sunny day, and people were stopping and listening, and Maddy was bowing and really enjoying the attention!
Interviewer:	And she still does?
Tanya:	Well, these days, years later, when I watch my daughter singing in front of a big crowd, there's always this curious thing – I suddenly realise that practically everyone is thinking that she's brilliant – it's not just me thinking, 'That's my little girl' – it's the whole room sharing the experience. It's not all roses, though. When Maddy had a bad patch with her singing career, she was taken on by a modelling agency.
Interviewer:	Another glamorous job.
Tanya:	Well, I don't think that modelling's at all easy. And I know she finds it hard when people back at the agency don't think she looks right for a particular job – you know she's too tall or something, or not young enough. It can be hard – even if, like Maddy, you know you're beautiful.

Interviewer: Mm, and how do you both deal with your fame?

Tanya: Well, we've talked about it – there is a certain look that people get on their faces when they recognise you, and I think probably that's what some people miss when they're no longer famous. But it also means that you can't go to the shops in peace. And that can be tough – so is reading about yourself in the paper, when what's being said is a load of rubbish. But you just have to learn to cope with that side of it …

[pause]

Now you'll hear Part Four again.

tone

[The recording is repeated.]

[pause]

That's the end of Part Four.

There'll now be a pause of five minutes for you to copy your answers onto the separate answer sheet. Be sure to follow the numbering of all the questions. I'll remind you when there is one minute left so that you are sure to finish in time.

[Teacher, pause the recording here for five minutes. Remind your students when they have one minute left.]

That's the end of the test. Please stop now. Your supervisor will now collect all the question papers and answer sheets.

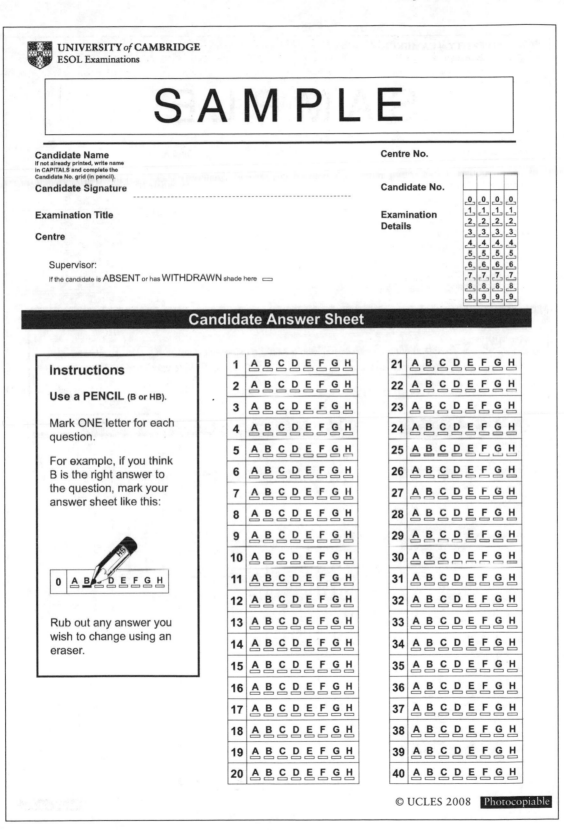

UNIVERSITY *of* CAMBRIDGE
ESOL Examinations

SAMPLE

Candidate Name
If not already printed, write name
in CAPITALS and complete the
Candidate No. grid (in pencil).

Candidate Signature

Examination Title

Centre

Supervisor:
If the candidate is ABSENT or has WITHDRAWN shade here ⊐

Centre No.

Candidate No.

Examination Details

Candidate Answer Sheet

Instructions
Use a PENCIL (B or HB). Rub out any answer you wish to change using an eraser.

Part 1: Mark ONE letter for each question.

For example, if you think **B** is the right answer to the question, mark your answer sheet like this:

0 A B C D

Parts 2, 3 and **4:** Write your answer clearly in CAPITAL LETTERS.

For Parts 2 and 3 write one letter in each box. For example:

0 E X A M P L E

Part 1

1	A	B	C	D
2	A	B	C	D
3	A	B	C	D
4	A	B	C	D
5	A	B	C	D
6	A	B	C	D
7	A	B	C	D
8	A	B	C	D
9	A	B	C	D
10	A	B	C	D
11	A	B	C	D
12	A	B	C	D

Part 2

Do not write below here

13	13 1 0 u
14	14 1 0 u
15	15 1 0 u
16	16 1 0 u
17	17 1 0 u
18	18 1 0 u
19	19 1 0 u
20	20 1 0 u
21	21 1 0 u
22	22 1 0 u
23	23 1 0 u
24	24 1 0 u

Continues over ➡

© UCLES 2008 Photocopiable

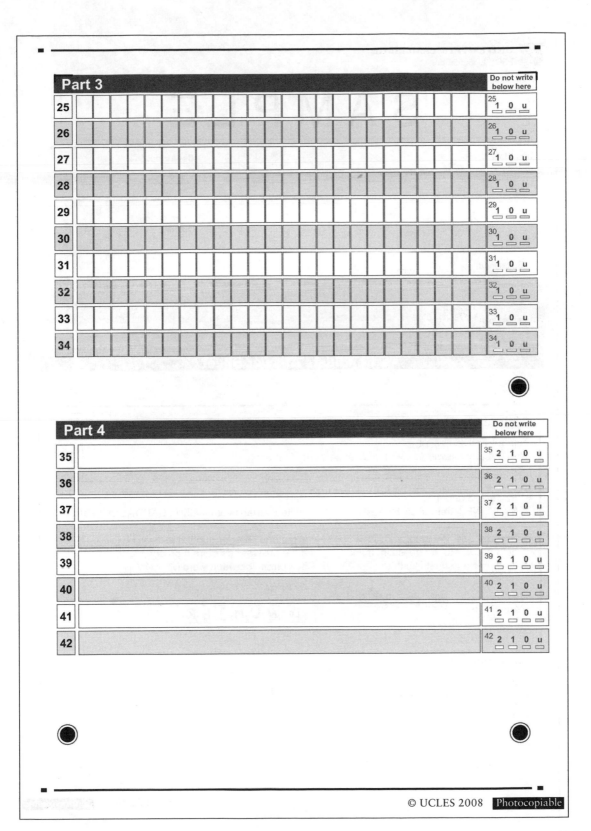

© UCLES 2008 Photocopiable

UNIVERSITY *of* CAMBRIDGE
ESOL Examinations

SAMPLE

Candidate Name
If not already printed, write name
in CAPITALS and complete the
Candidate No. grid (in pencil).

Candidate Signature

Examination Title

Centre

Supervisor:

If the candidate is ABSENT or has WITHDRAWN shade here

Test version: A B C D E F J K L M N

Special arrangements: S H

Centre No.

Candidate No.

**Examination
Details**

0	0	0	0
1	1	1	1
2	2	2	2
3	3	3	3
4	4	4	4
5	5	5	5
6	6	6	6
7	7	7	7
8	8	8	8
9	9	9	9

Candidate Answer Sheet

Instructions

Use a PENCIL (B or HB).
Rub out any answer you wish to change using an eraser.

Parts 1, 3 and **4:**
Mark ONE letter for each question.

For example, if you think **B** is the
right answer to the question, mark
your answer sheet like this:

0 A B C

Part 2:
Write your answer clearly in CAPITAL LETTERS.

Write one letter or number in each box.
If the answer has more than one word, leave one
box empty between words.

For example:

0 N U M B E R   1 2

Turn this sheet over to start.

© UCLES 2008 Photocopiable

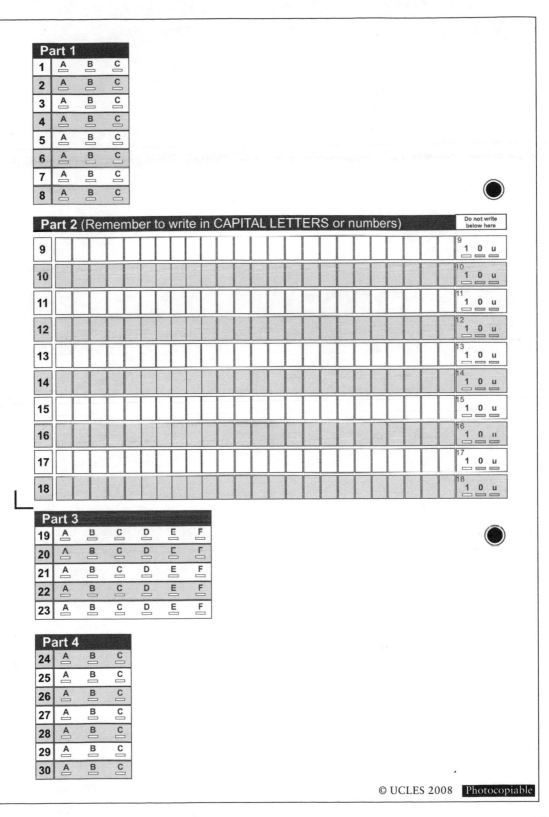

© UCLES 2008   Photocopiable